Arturo Toscanini

Arturo Toscanini

Denis Matthews
with selected discography by Ray Burford

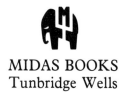

MIDAS BOOKS
Tunbridge Wells

HIPPOCRENE BOOKS
New York

In the same illustrated series
Sir Adrian Boult by Nigel Simeone and Simon Mundy
Maria Callas by Carla Verga
John Ireland by Muriel Searle
Niccolo Paganini—Supreme Violinist or Devil's Fidler? by John Sugden
Leopold Stokowski by Preben Opperby
Edited by Robert Hardcastle

In the Midas Composers: Life and Times series:
Bach by Tim Dowley
Bartok by Hamish Milne
Beethoven by Ates Orga
Chopin by Ates Orga
Dvorak by Neil Butterworth
Elgar by Simon Mundy
Haydn by Neil Butterworth
Mahler by Edward Seckerson
Mendelssohn by Mozelle Moshansky
Mozart by Peggy Woodford
Offenbach by Peter Gammond
Rachmaninoff by Robert Walker
Shostakovich by Eric Roseberry
Schubert by Peggy Woodford
Schumann by Tim Dowley
Tchaikovsky by Wilson Strutte
Verdi by Peter Southwell-Sander

First published UK in 1982 by
MIDAS BOOKS
12 Dene Way, Speldhurst,
Tunbridge Wells, Kent TN3 0NX

ISBN 0 85936 172 1 (UK)

First published USA in 1982 by
HIPPOCRENE BOOKS INC
171 Madison Avenue,
New York, NY 10016

ISBN 0 88254 657 0 (US)

Printed and bound in Great Britain by
The Pitman Press, Bath.

CONTENTS

	Preface	7
1	From Parma to La Scala	11
2	The Years at the Met	27
3	Return to La Scala	38
4	Bayreuth and Salzburg	49
5	Toscanini in London	64
6	The NBC Symphony	77
7	'Ritorni Toscanini'	93
8	Toscanini and the Critics	103
9	Postscript	119
	References	123
	A Selected Discography	125
	General Notes	168
	Index	171

ACKNOWLEDGEMENTS

The first acknowledgement must be made to the inspiring nature of the subject of this monograph. Plenty of others have been inspired to write about Toscanini, and special debts are due to those who have been liberally quoted and to others listed in the bibliography. Most of those who heard, knew, or worked with the Maestro have been only too eager to share and pass on their experiences. Among them I must thank players from the BBC, the Philharmonia and the NBC orchestras. Others whose memories of Toscanini have helped me in the writing of these pages have included Sir Adrian Boult, Dame Myra Hess, Ernest Newman and Dr Rudolf Schwarz. I am also grateful to Ray Burford and Thomas Heinitz for their interest and enthusiasm and for drawing my attention to some of the lesser-known and unpublished recordings.

Editor's Note

In November of each year the Torbay Gramophone Society runs a musical week-end at the Palace Hotel in Torquay. These are always delightful occasions, but 1978 was especially memorable for me because I was able to bring together two of my friends who share a profound and inextinguishable enthusiasm for the work of Arturo Toscanini, and suggest to them that they should work together on a new book about the great Italian conductor. The fruits of that first meeting are to found in these pages.

On behalf of the publishers I would like to thank RCA for their kind permission to reproduce many of the illustrations in this volume. I am also greatly indebted to Toscanini's granddaughter, Emanuela Castelbarco, for so generously making available a number of unique photographs from her private collection.   RFH

PREFACE

The following pages, whatever their shortcomings, will be above all a labour of love. They come in profound gratitude for many incomparable musical experiences and for the enduring example of one man's tireless quest for an unattainable perfection. The degree of devotion and affection that Toscanini inspired in others through his own passionate involvement with his work was unique in his time – probably in any time, considering the fairly late emergence in musical history of the conductor as interpreter. This is to discount completely those elements of slavish loyalty and fanaticism that so often follow in the wake of famous people, though Toscanini certainly had more than a fair share of these. Loyalty and fanaticism may be touchingly human expressions of devotion but they are notorious underminers of objective criticism. Toscanini was a fanatic himself in the highest degree but of an altogether legitimate kind. It has been claimed that objectivity was the very essence of his art, though in this context the term is ambiguous and debatable. The composer Alfredo Casella, whose works Toscanini never actually played, wrote instead of his 'absolute, ideal impersonality'. He carried with him an unquenchable desire for music-making of the utmost unanimity, eloquence and fidelity. Such an aim may be claimed by countless artists, but in Toscanini's case extraordinary gifts produced extraordinary results, causing one to reassess the whole nature and possibilities of the performer's responsibility to the composer. At times his discontent may have seemed far from divine, and there were always a few who to their own loss wrote him off as a tyrant and a dangerous influence. A legendary reputation is a danger in itself, carrying the seeds of prejudice and blind acceptance. But how did the reputation arise?

Most of those who heard and worked with him must have felt something quite unaccountable, almost supernatural and godlike about Toscanini's powers. Even his most esteemed colleagues had to search for words. Klemperer spoke of 'a miracle', Monteux of 'a real revelation' and Weingartner of an 'undreamt-of perfection'. Bruno Walter told Sir Adrian Boult that for him Toscanini was 'like a great high-priest of music, caring only for beauty and the mind of the composer.' Such comments from responsible critics could be gathered a hundredfold throughout the whole length and breadth of his remarkable career. They do not or should not imply for one moment that he was somehow infallible or beyond criticism. Others have delighted in pointing to the serious defects of his virtues on occasion, and no true admirer of Toscanini could claim that he had no human failings or stylistic limitations. There was the further danger that his overwhelming qualities should be looked for and missed elsewhere. An eternal yardstick! His London performances of the Verdi *Requiem* in 1938 were described at the time as 'supreme in conception and magnificent in execution, by which standards can be corrected and others judged.' I was present in the Queen's Hall and can concur with every word, but inevitably even more sweeping claims were made. It is all the more sad that they bred scepticism and downright denigration in other quarters. There was bound to be partisanship too. A player in the Berlin Philharmonic, Furtwängler's orchestra, was heard to dismiss Toscanini as '*that* is not music.'

Like any other human being Toscanini was bound inescapably by his own knowledge, taste and temperament, by the age and environment into which he was born and – though this is often exaggerated – by his nationality. This obvious statement does not lessen his achievements but makes them even more remarkable when we consider the wide range of his sympathies. Beecham, who was expectedly hostile to the Toscanini cult in general, was forced to concede that he was a very good conductor of Italian opera. Rossini, Verdi, Puccini: Toscanini's gifts were nurtured in the opera-house and would presumably thrive first of all on home ground. But Verdi *and* Wagner, Wagner *and* Brahms? Debussy, Richard Strauss, Elgar, Sibelius? These all figure in my own list of revelations, and they were all composers of the new music for which he fought in his youth, a part of the Toscanini story that is too often undertold or forgotten. As for the earlier classics, Beethoven, 'that saint' as he called him, is bound to figure largely in any discussion of Toscanini's art. His love of Haydn is well known, but his general approach to Mozart has always been a bone of contention even among his most ardent devotees. There were, I think, historical and temperamental reasons for his sometimes brusque and relentless treatment of a composer who was too often prettified in the Romantic age.

Yet this reaction against accepted and easy-going traditions was also at the root of Toscanini's greatness. He would have agreed with Mahler that 'tradition is laziness'. No-one can of course be completely aloof from it, since in a sense tradition is the main stream that makes music a vital means of communication. How was it running in the days of Toscanini's youth? There is plenty of evidence to suggest that it was notoriously muddy in places. The self-aggrandisement of the virtuoso and the prima donna at the expense of the composer was matched by a cavalier attitude to the text. From the start of his career Toscanini established a new era of respect for the score. His own saying 'play as written' may have been a misleading half-truth, yet there were countless times when some astonishing new light in a familiar work derived from a scrupulous observation of the composer's marks. George Szell called Toscanini a truth-seeker, but can 'truth' be said to exist in artistic matters and if so can it be anything but elusive and arguable? Ideas and ideals of authenticity are constantly on the move, and many composers have accepted varied readings of their works. Think back to Mozart and our modern desires to recapture the 'authentic' Mozartian sound: would we recommend playing his C major Symphony K338 with forty violins, ten double-basses, six bassoons and the rest to match? Yet Mozart wrote from Vienna in 1781 that 'it went magnifique'.

With these thoughts in mind it is instructive to listen again to Toscanini's old 1929 recording of Haydn's 'Clock' Symphony. Not that he used such extravagant forces, except that the string section was probably larger than is normally approved today. The point is that in terms of balance and finesse and the overall architectural sense that was his own secret he achieved a perfection or near-perfection that endures. Purists who quibble over his correction of a supposed mistake in the string harmonies of the trio in the minuet might note that he re-corrected them in later performances! All this however was inevitably within his own aesthetic. Tastes may change, influenced by research and knowledge and the swing of the pendulum; but it may be argued that what counts most is the 'inner truth' of a performance, in which every detail is heard in proportion. When an entire opera, even the full span of *Die Meistersinger,* is presented with such integration and subtlety and apparent spontaneity, with such command of every strand of its texture and no trace of self-indulgence on the part of the interpreter, we are faced with the genius that was Toscanini. That is why he remains a talking-point after all these years and why yet another book about him comes to be written. If he is also a frequent arguing-point so much the better, for what genius in whatever walk of life has not provoked controversies?

Toscanini objected to the word genius being applied to himself or to any other mere interpreter of music. Genius resides in a Beethoven symphony or a Verdi opera, and in this light the performers are no more than the composer's humble servants. When Sir Adrian Boult first introduced him to the BBC Symphony Orchestra in 1935 and in glowing terms Toscanini's immediate reaction was 'no, no, no, no, no – not that at all – just an honest musician!' This was not false modesty. Toscanini disliked applause and shunned publicity all his life, though he received far more of both than those who courted them. Much of the publicity was admittedly only indirectly concerned with music: the stories of his intransigence, of his battles with singers and orchestras and even with the public, of his defiance of Mussolini and Hitler – and of his legendary memory. None of this would have had news value if he had not also been in universal demand as an artist in a kind of class of his own. Even to this day, sayings like 'not even Toscanini' or 'who does he think he is – Toscanini?' are to be heard in band-rooms all over the world.

Although Toscanini's art remains vivid through his recordings it must be stressed that most of them only represent the very last phase of his long life's work. For years he fought shy of recording, though a few classics survive from the vintage period of his own sixties and early seventies: his 1929 and 1936 sessions with the New York Philharmonic-Symphony, followed by those with the BBC in London. In 1938 there began the long series with the NBC in New York by which he is largely known today. The earlier NBC records were appalling in quality, largely due to the dry acoustics of the notorious Studio 8H in Radio City, and it is ironic that snap judgments of Toscanini used to be made on these by people who had never heard the splendour of his sound in the flesh. Fortunately things improved as he agreed to make more and more recordings in his old age, and continuing interest in Toscanini has led to far more recent issues, like the salvaging of his wonderful but ill-fated records with the Philadelphia Orchestra. Unofficial ones have appeared, taken from broadcasts and some of them going back to the mid-1930s. These ghosts from the past, even when dimly discerned, are of immense value. They afford interesting comparisons in an art that was never static, and for older generations they also serve as memory-checks. Yes, the 1937 *Falstaff* and *Meistersinger* at Salzburg were as miraculous as one recalled, and *The Magic Flute* seems just as strangely unidiomatic. One thing is certain: the widespread orchestral virtuosity of today, coupled with the most advanced recording techniques, cannot replace the mind, ear and heart of a Toscanini. This is not to deny that the subtle tyranny of the microphone had its effect on him also in his later years. His recordings are bound to come in for discussion in relation to his life-story and my own Toscanini memories, but I am glad that Ray Burford is to deal with them in more specific detail. He has a vast knowledge of them and their availability and shares my unbounded enthusiasm for the subject.

The enthusiasm in my own case dates back to Toscanini's first visit to the BBC Orchestra in the summer of 1935. I heard all the four concerts on the air. Sir John Barbirolli was in the Queen's Hall for the first of them and wrote afterwards: 'It is extraordinary how a man of such individual power can yet create the illusion that there is nothing coming between you and the music.' That in brief was the most baffling and the most wonderful thing about Toscanini. It is hard to describe musical phenomena in words, and in his case there is the recurring problem that superlatives may run dry or become counter-productive. In any case the effort must be made to produce a balanced assessment. The extraordinary story of Toscanini's career has been told many times and most recently by Harvey Sachs, whose well-researched book *Toscanini* (1978) has thrown much new light on the various stages of his life and with admirable objectivity. Debts will obviously be made to Mr Sachs and other writers such as Howard Taubman and Filippo Sacchi, but the following is also based on many personal experiences, thoughts and memories, and the desire to hand them down.

DENIS MATTHEWS

Newcastle upon Tyne
1980

Chapter One

FROM PARMA
TO LA SCALA

In November 1939, while America was enjoying a precarious neutrality in the early stages of the Hitler war, *Life* magazine came out with a feature on Toscanini showing him in a relaxed mood with his five-year-old granddaughter Sonia Horowitz. This picture scoop, as the editor called it, conflicted with the usual image of the great conductor whose tantrums struck fear into the toughest orchestras and who had defied both the German and Italian dictators. With Sonia he was content to play hide-and-seek, to give her a piano lesson, and even to take a lesson *from* her in conducting. She was however the daughter of a world-famous pianist, whereas Toscanini (we were told) had had no music in his family: 'his father was an unmusical tailor; his mother was an unmusical housewife.' This was effective journalese, on the lines that a phenomenon is all the more phenomenal when completely unaccounted for. But Toscanini had at least grown up in an atmosphere where music, and especially opera, was taken for granted as an important extension of life. He was born at Parma in Italy, where the local opera-house was above average and well spoken of by Verdi himself. His unmusical father Claudio was musical enough to sing in the chorus from time to time. His mother Paolina may have been a severely practical woman with little time for art, but she came from a family of music-lovers. One of Toscanini's earliest memories was of being taken by his maternal grandfather, or perhaps his uncle, to hear Verdi's *Un Ballo in Maschera* at the age of four. This he recalled eighty-three years later when he conducted the work during his last NBC season in New York.

Toscanini's father had allegiances quite apart from his family and his tailoring. He had been a supporter of Garibaldi's revolutionary army from the start, had been imprisoned and narrowly escaped execution before he met Paolina Montani. He was still liable to rush off at the drop of a hat or the sign of a red shirt, and even his honeymoon was dramatically cut short by a call to duty. Some of this fanatical devotion to a cause was inherited by his first-born, the Arturo we know and can never forget. Although Arturo was to take charge of the family during his earlier career, his parents and younger sisters soon recede from view in accounts of his life. Claudio lived to witness his son as head of La Scala in Milan, and Paolina, who died in 1924, outlived her husband by eighteen years. The picture of her as a stubborn and embittered woman did not change however, and in the days of Toscanini's childhood she seemed determined to save the face of the family in spite of Claudio's erratic ways. Arturo said later that he never knew whether his mother really loved him or in some perverse way resented his success.

Toscanini was born on 25 March 1867 and it is worth putting the date into musical perspective. Verdi had just composed *Don Carlos* but not yet *Aida,* Wagner was finishing the scoring of *Die Meistersinger,* and Brahms had nine years to go before launching his First Symphony. Debussy was four and Puccini eight. He was to serve all these composers with comparable devotion. As an Italian his love and understanding of Verdi were to be expected, and during his formative years the Wagner-Brahms controversy was at its height. It seemed significant that at the very end of his career Toscanini should make his last appearance in London with two Brahms concerts and take his final leave in New York with an all-Wagner programme.

The story of Toscanini's childhood has been sketched in several biographies, not helped by his own reluctance to write or talk about his career except to a few close friends. One such friend was Filippo Sacchi, whose book *The Magic Baton* conjured up the early Parma scene in some detail. It seems clear that as a child Toscanini was serious and sensitive and, if needs be, as stubborn as his mother. The qualities of extreme sensitivity and obsessive determination were at the heart of his character and could in their nature form a dangerously explosive mixture. A gift soon noted was his remarkable memory, later described by Busoni as 'a phenomenon in the annals of physiology'. Toscanini never conducted from a score in his life, and his bad eye-sight is usually given as a contributory reason. That astonishing feat should not sway musical judgment, but neither could Toscanini be blamed for creating a fetish. His memory was the servant and symptom of his concentration and an enormous asset in physical communication. It showed early on in his ability to remember a poem after one reading and to pick out tunes from operas on his school-teacher's piano. By the age of nine his musical leanings were obvious and he was accepted first as a day-boy and then as a living-in scholar at the Parma Conservatory, where life was spartan and strictly regulated. He learnt rudiments, harmony and musical history, played the piano and the cello, and was made to take the latter as his first instrument. As with many students at such academies he gained much valuable musical experience by his own initiative. He broke the rules, sold his food to buy scores, and gathered together groups of fellow-students for informal and secret music-making. His knowledge and critical sense led to the nickname of 'genio' or genius, which he detested, but he had already proved his power to organise and direct. He also composed a good deal and conducted one of his works at an official concert. It is said that he was never taught to conduct, but he had plenty of opportunities of observing and assimilating. As a cellist he was required to play with other advanced students in the orchestra at the Teatro Regio and thus got to know the workings and the repertory of an opera-house from the inside.

Toscanini with his granddaughter Sonia Horowitz.

Toscanini's birthplace at Parma in northern Italy.

The repertory, unlike that of most opera-houses today, was based on new and recent works with a natural preference for Italian composers. Toscanini did not come across *Figaro* or *Fidelio* or *Der Freischütz* at the Regio, but the latest opera by Verdi or indeed some far lesser composer had the attraction of a new 'musical' and its tunes were soon heard in the streets. In 1884, however, *Lohengrin* was produced, and Toscanini immediately fell under the spell of Wagner's genius from the very opening of the Prelude with its 'celestial harmonies.' Playing the cello in five seasons of opera was at least a good preparation for the adventure that followed on his graduation from the Conservatory. The news of his all-round musicianship had spread, and when the impresario Rossi engaged him to go with a travelling opera company to South America he acquired in Toscanini a first cellist, an assistant chorus-master, and a coach for the solo singers. It was natural enough that the company should turn to him in an emergency. The story of that emergency and the triumph that followed has often been told. His whole career was

Toscanini at the age of 8 years, with his aunt Clementina and his sister Cesira. The following year he started his studies at the Parma Conservatory.

prone to dramatic incidents and departures, but nothing could have been more dramatic than Toscanini's unexpected conducting début in Rio de Janeiro.

The crisis arose over *Aida*, with the Brazilian conductor Miguez resigning and the Italian deputy shouted off by a hostile and chauvinistic audience. The singers turned in desperation to Toscanini, who was shy to intervene but was eventually persuaded. His youthful appearance quietened the tumult, he conducted the entire opera without looking at the score, turned an imminent tragedy into artistic triumph, and saved the company from financial disaster. 'I didn't have the technique, but I conducted' he said later. The astonishment

15

of his colleagues was shared by the public and the press, which wrote already about 'a sure-handed and secure conductor' and 'sacred artistic fire'. It is obvious that Toscanini had never conducted an opera before and astounding that he did so from memory and without rehearsal, but it is also clear that in coaching and playing in *Aida* he had absorbed every note of the score. One outcome was that Rossi engaged him at once to take over the rest of the season – what alternative had he? – though he conveniently forgot to raise his salary. The repertory included a further ten different operas, and in view of this remarkable assignment it may seem trivial to mention that at a benefit concert given for him in Rio he conducted a minuet by Bolzoni. The critic of *O Pais* observed that 'it could not have been played with greater polish.' We know all about this quality from the later Toscanini, but at nineteen, with a touring orchestra and eleven operas suddenly thrust upon him, it seems that the power of instant communication was already at work.

Toscanini found no hero's welcome on his return to Italy, nor did he expect one. He was not the person to brag about his South American exploits and he saw no prospect of conducting in his homeland. The Russian tenor Nicolai Figner, who had been with him in Rio, did not however forget. He sent Toscanini his fare to Milan, where he and his wife were staying, got him to coach them in various operatic parts, and by a ruse introduced him to the composer Alfredo Catalani, whose opera *Edmea* was to be produced in Turin. In that same year of 1886, which had seen his Brazilian successes, Toscanini made his Italian début with *Edmea*. It was the beginning of a long association with Turin and of a close friendship with Catalani that was cut short by his early death seven years later. By that time Toscanini had conducted two more of his operas, *Loreley* and *La Wally* (after which his elder daughter was to be named), and he continued to play extracts from these in much later years. Catalani's gratitude was boundless and once again the critics were tongue-tied, falling back on 'indescribable' as the ultimate epithet. Although a Milan paper wrote of the *Edmea* performance as 'a splendid dawn on the artistic horizon' it was nine years before Toscanini found himself with a regular post at the Teatro Regio in Turin. He accepted engagements where and when he found them: in Casale Monferrato, Genoa, Verona, at the Teatro Dal Verme in Milan, in Palermo, Rome and many smaller Italian cities – and in Barcelona. The repertory he took on was formidable, bearing in mind that he really knew and weighed up every note of every opera he conducted. He already showed a growing independence from tradition, began to impose his will on singers, players and impresarios, and defied the public by refusing to grant encores.

For a year or two after *Edmea* he did not however confine himself to conducting. He still composed a little, mostly songs, and he continued to play the cello. His first hearing of *Tristan*, which Martucci conducted at Bologna in 1888, put an end to any aspirations he may have had as a composer, but his intense love for Wagner in no way inhibited his devotion to Verdi. In the

16

previous year he had joined the orchestra of La Scala as second cellist in order to take part, however unobtrusively, in the first performance of *Otello*. Toscanini's unobtrusiveness brought him face to face with Verdi, who was supervising the rehearsals and who asked him to 'play louder' in the famous passage for four cellos towards the end of the first act. He was surprised because he thought he was following the written dynamics, and the rest of the story has been told in different ways: that Verdi admitted Toscanini was right but said with resignation that 'he had better go along with the others'; that with orchestras of the time Verdi had to write a triple *piano* to get one *piano;* and that he wanted a warm singing quality even in the quietest playing. In any case it was a lesson Toscanini never forgot. When rehearsing *Un Ballo in Maschera* in 1954 he told the NBC players that 'in Verdi you *sing* the melody always – is not Beethoven, is not Wagner – is not even Mozart!' His full-blooded treatment of the first string entry in the overture to *La Forza del Destino* was another example, though his call for 'sempre cantare' was by no means confined to Verdi!

Although Toscanini was overwhelmed by the music of *Otello* he must have had serious doubts about the justice done to it. He had already shown at the age of twenty that his own standards were high, and as an itinerant free-lance he was to learn about the problems of achieving them. He was freed from tradition when he introduced new works like Leoncavallo's *I Pagliacci,* but had to fight preconceptions and complacency when he conducted established ones. In 1894 he gave *Otello* himself at Pisa and Verdi's still later *Falstaff* in Treviso and Bologna. *Falstaff* produced an argument with the singer Pini-Corsi who had been coached in the part of Ford by Verdi the previous year, but when Verdi was consulted over a matter of tempo he said Pini-Corsi had already forgotten what he had taught him. This confirmed Toscanini's general principle that the score should take precedence over doubtful word-of-mouth traditions: a singer might tell his pupils not one but forty years later that he had had it 'straight from Verdi'.

The one great composer Toscanini had little chance of conducting in those early years was Wagner. He had been pleased to take over a rehearsal of *The Flying Dutchman* for Alessandra Pomé in Turin in 1886, and had directed the work in 1893 during a season at Palermo, where he ran into audience trouble over encores and for a change received some hostile notices. But the later and greater Wagner? A turning-point came when Giuseppe Depanis, a lawyer and critic who had watched Toscanini's career and shared his ideals, persuaded the city of Turin to offer him a permanent post at its Teatro Regio. His reputation was now such that he was entrusted with the forming of a new orchestra, with which he was soon conducting concerts as well, and it is significant that he chose to open his inaugural season at the end of 1895 with the first-ever Italian production of *Die Götterdämmerung.* Since the run of an opera depended on its popular success it is astounding to note that it received twenty-one performances that season. He made some cuts, not surprisingly in

An early studio portrait of Toscanini in 1896 – the year of the world premiere of Puccini's *La Bohème*. It was also an important year for the young conductor: he gave his first symphony concert (in Turin) and fulfilled his first engagement at La Scala, Milan, where he conducted four orchestral concerts.

view of the work's unfamiliarity and colossal time-scale. If this strikes one as sacrilege the answer is that in those days and to an Italian audience it was better than not performing it at all. Even at Leipzig, Mendelssohn had been forced to reduce the great C major Symphony of Schubert by half its length in order to put it across. Pioneers may have to temper purism, and Toscanini was in every sense a pioneer in Italy in the eighteen-nineties.

An important première during his first Turin season was of Puccini's *La Bohème*. The critics praised Toscanini but not the work, though its growing popularity proved their forecasts wrong; and the occasion marked the beginning of Puccini's on-and-off friendship with his 'highly intelligent' interpreter. Another lasting and less precarious relationship was with Arrigo Boito, composer of *Mefistofele* and librettist for Verdi's *Otello* and *Falstaff*. Boito admired Toscanini's conducting of both Verdi and Wagner and was to be an influence behind his appointment to La Scala in 1898. Meanwhile the many operas produced at Turin included Toscanini's first *Tristan,* and he showed his lack of partisanship by giving the first performance in Italy of Brahms's Tragic Overture in a symphony concert with the new orchestra. His success in this new field was immediate. Curiously and in the longest term prophetically it was as a symphonic conductor that La Scala first heard him in 1896 in four concerts: 'A theatre such as we have never seen before: completely sold out . . . great applause for all the pieces', which included, by the way, the great Schubert C major mentioned above. In ten years and while still in his twenties Toscanini's name had become a household word even in opera-houses where he had not conducted before. The path to the directorship of La Scala had been cleared, though the way was not easy. Toscanini had also acquired a reputation of being 'difficult', of cancelling or postponing a performance if his demands were not met, of walking out on a contract, and even of venting his rage on the music if audiences misbehaved.

Toscanini's temper, about which stories are legion, was inextricably bound up with his abnormal powers of concentration. Those who wished to make music in an easy-going or half-hearted way might do so elsewhere, but not with him. Harvey Sachs has written about a dichotomy in his character that developed during these hard-working and formative years:[1]

> According to all reports of people who knew him in his youth, he was shy and quiet by nature, and many who knew him in later years felt the same was true then. No matter: the music was of such overriding importance to him that he would do whatever had to be done to upset the lethargy of routine. . . . And so the twist in his personality developed, a twist he himself resented and perhaps often regretted, but did not renounce. He could rehearse patiently for hours when he felt everyone was working at highest capacity; but when he suspected less than one hundred per cent cooperation he became a monster. Something in him would snap. . . .

Sir Adrian Boult, who got to know his working methods well during the nineteen-thirties, spoke indeed of his patience at rehearsal, and his economy: he would cut a rehearsal short or even cancel one if things went well. Boult also remarked that his concentration was such that an earthquake could not have dislodged it; but if musical things went wrong and repeatedly wrong he was liable to provide an earthquake of his own. There was nothing egotistic about his outbursts and most players and singers came to accept them as a necessary safety-valve, but Toscanini wrote in those early years of his misery over the involuntary embitterments he caused. His touchiness, call it extreme sensitivity or obstinacy, was known however to invade his private life as well and sometimes in seemingly petty ways.

In 1897 Toscanini married Carla de Martini, whose sister Ida had been one of the Rhinemaidens in the Turin *Götterdämmerung*. Although the marriage lasted until her death in 1951, Carla's lot can never have been an easy one. Toscanini in any case had strict views about the contractual nature of marriage. He disapproved strongly of divorce, and it took him years to reconcile himself to his daughter Wally's wedding with Count Castelbarco who left his first wife for her. Yet he was quite incapable of withstanding his own susceptibilities, and two of his affairs had serious consequences. Both of them involved opera-singers. Rosina Storchio had a son by him in 1903, and in 1915 Geraldine Farrar tried to persuade him to leave his family for her. He left the New York Metropolitan instead. Even Carla's wedding-day was a nightmare. Toscanini had planned a quiet out-of-town ceremony, but the news leaked out and they were greeted with cheering crowds. This conflict with his vision of the day was intolerable. Something snapped: his obstinacy, so often a source of strength in artistic matters, could be a trial to family and friends, even though Carla would later admit that she was proud and content to be the wife of 'this one man'. All this is not irrelevant to a discussion of Toscanini's musical career. A price might have to be paid for the unbelievable rewards of his obsessive genius, and La Scala was soon to learn about it.

When he arrived there in 1898 he was still only thirty-one. His new general manager, Gatti-Casazza, was even younger, all of which disturbed the traditionalists but promised renewed vitality at the fountain-head of the Italian musical scene. As at Turin, Toscanini opened with Wagner. This time it was *Die Meistersinger*, another massive undertaking that proved a resounding success: better, according to Giulio Ricordi, than anything to be heard elsewhere, even at Bayreuth. Toscanini's demands for control over everything – orchestra, choice of singers, rehearsals, stage, lighting – had yielded immediate results. The musical effect might still have been stunning even without such preparation, as happened with *Aida* at Rio, but he could now pursue his ideals further. When he saw them frustrated, however, the result could be disastrous diplomatically and financially. The next opera, *Norma*, was cancelled at the final rehearsal. The title-role is demanding vocally and complex emotionally, but Toscanini had chosen his singer and then found her wanting. He would accept no compromise, and this gave plenty of fuel to his detractors. Once again he was the genius or the upstart, and these opposing attitudes were to persist in varying degrees and dilutions. Boito was dismayed but understanding, but Ricordi's earlier praise gave way to a campaign of hostility. They were both friends of Verdi, who thus received conflicting views of Toscanini's *Falstaff*.

As the librettist of *Falstaff* Boito's enthusiasm must have carried some weight, but Ricordi now began a series of complaints about Toscanini's 'rigidity'. Verdi unfortunately never heard him conduct a note of his own music, though he had applauded him in Franchetti's *Cristoforo Colombo* at Genoa in 1892 and was to take his side again when a dispute over tempi arose with Tamagno during rehearsals of *Otello*. Toscanini had also been to see him about the *Te Deum* and over a matter not of strictness but of freedom of tempo. He felt a *rallentando* was called for where none was written, and Verdi agreed that the true musician must know where to read between the lines, since a printed instruction would easily be exaggerated. So much for Ricordi's 'rigidity'!

Toscanini's second season at La Scala seemed to dismiss the Wagner *or* Verdi argument for good by opening with *Siegfried* and continuing the next night with *Otello*. Considering the high pitch of concentration at which he worked, his energies and his memory were still astounding. Early in 1900 he followed *Otello* with *Lohengrin* and then with three operas new to Milan: the world première of Galeotti's *Anton*, the Milanese première of *Tosca*, and the first Italian production of *Eugene Onegin*. He conducted orchestral concerts and took the Scala orchestra on a tour that included his native Parma. The musical world outside Italy soon heard of these events, and in 1901 Wagner's son Siegfried went to La Scala to hear Toscanini conduct *Tristan*. He was so enthusiastic on his return to Bayreuth that his mother Cosima wrote to Toscanini:[2]

> My son stressed the meticulous zeal which you brought to the orchestral preparations and the excellent result obtained by this zeal, along with your ability as conductor. He also told me that the singers knew their roles perfectly and delivered them with passion and enthusiasm.

She added that Siegfried had been impressed by the attention and 'intelligent liveliness' of the audience. In spite of this it was nearly thirty years before Toscanini was invited to conduct at Bayreuth, and the effect of his 'meticulous zeal' at the Wagner shrine itself must form part of a muc̈ later chapter. Meanwhile his travels in the off-season took him much further afield. In the summer of 1901, far from taking a vacation, he returned to South America and conducted no less than fifteen different operas in Buenos Aires. One of them was *La Traviata*, and back at La Scala he decided that the time had come to look afresh at the earlier Verdi operas. They had long suffered from their own popularity, the victims of casual and slapdash performance and of singers' liberties, which in turn had led to a patronising attitude from more serious opera-goers.

The fourth Scala season (1901-2) had opened yet again with Wagner, this time *Die Walküre*. It was also the first season after the death of Verdi. Toscanini conducted the *Requiem* for the first time and electrified the audience with the 'Dies Irae', as he was always to do, and he then applied himself to the task of rediscovering *Il Trovatore*, not as usually heard or half-heard but as Verdi had written it. This was the performance that Ricordi,

Toscanini married Carla de Martini on June 21st 1897. This photograph, taken in Buenos Aires in 1904, shows him with their first child, Walter.

Verdi's publisher, tried to prevent on the grounds that Toscanini was about to tamper with a comfortable tradition and therefore, presumably, with the spirit of the composer. Ricordi failed and Toscanini triumphed, though the real triumph was in fact Verdi's, as a war-horse of the repertory was suddenly revalued. Criticisms from that time make it clear that Toscanini's abundant gifts of musicianship, communication, determination and humility were wholly at the service of the composer. We read of his artistic honesty, that he was faithful and simple before Verdi as he was before Wagner, and of his unique power of 'bringing into relief every smallest detail'. He had already won a lasting place in the annals of operatic history, and in the purely orchestral field he continued to introduce new works with incomparable advocacy.

One such work was *Till Eulenspiegel,* which was encored. In opera, however, encores were another matter, altogether disruptive of continuity and symbolic of the vanity of singers; but the demand for a *bis* was the deeply ingrained prerogative of Italian audiences. Toscanini even walked out when the public refused to allow him to continue with Weber's *Euryanthe* without repeating the overture, and broke with La Scala, apparently for good, over unruly audience reaction concerning a *bis* in *Un Ballo in Maschera* in 1903. His abrupt departure for Argentina may have seemed a gesture of defiance but had already been planned to follow the end of the Scala season. Buenos Aires wanted him back and he took most of his productions there to Montevideo as well. For two years he was a free-lance again.

On his return to Italy he conducted orchestral concerts in Bologna, Rome and Turin and studied more new scores. Some works, like Strauss's *Domestic Symphony* and Mahler's *Fifth*, he felt unable to perform and his letters to friends are full of well-reasoned opinions. He never played a note of Mahler, only took to a handful of works by Tchaikowsky and Dvorak, and his tastes were sometimess influenced by personal affection for less-known composers like Catalani and Martucci. Martucci was an enterprising all-round musician, to whom Toscanini owed his first hearing of *Tristan,* and who even conducted an entire programme of British music at Bologna in 1898, including Sullivan, Stanford and Parry. Seven years later, also at Bologna, Toscanini introduced Elgar's *Enigma,* a work he took to his heart and was to play often in later years, but his programmes there also included Sibelius's *En Saga* and Debussy's *L'Après-midi.* Nor did his great love of Wagner *and* Verdi prevent his growing enthusiasm for Brahms. He would have been great if he had only conducted Verdi as he did, and his grasp of a wide range of new idioms should never be forgotten by critics who fasten on to his supposed limitations. In addition, his detailed knowledge of works beyond his own repertory always impressed his fellow-musicians.

During his absence from La Scala two other conductors, Campanini and Mugnone, had taken over in turn, but when Toscanini made a brief reappearance there in 1905 for concerts with the Turin orchestra the public and press clamoured for his return. He threw himself into opera again with seasons in Bologna, Turin and Buenos Aires, and in 1906 it was announced that he would resume his directorship of La Scala later that year. He made strict conditions, including a ban on encores. This move from Turin to Milan, for the second time in eight years, soon produced a crisis over the first Italian performance of Strauss's *Salome,* which had been promised to Turin and which Toscanini now hoped to transfer to La Scala. In the outcome Strauss conducted the Turin première while Toscanini forestalled it by throwing open the dress rehearsal of his own Scala production the previous evening. The whole episode smacks of pettiness and obstinate misunderstandings. Toscanini never conducted a Strauss opera again, though the tone-poems like *Don Juan* became part of his regular repertory, and his mixed attitude was summed up thirty years later when Strauss appeared to accept and condone Nazi Germany: 'I take off my hat to you as a

23

A rare photograph of the conductor taken in 1903.

composer – as a man, I put back ten hats.' But Toscanini also admired Strauss as an interpreter, especially of Mozart. He was exalted when he heard him conduct *Figaro*, an opera he never performed himself.

It is strange that one of the greatest of all opera composers should figure so little in Toscanini's long list of productions. He played *Don Giovanni* at Buenos Aires in 1906, prepared but withdrew it at La Scala in 1929, and produced *Die Zauberflöte* only twice in his whole career, in 1923 and 1937. 'There is something missing in me' he once said on the subject of Mozart. The notion that he was basically a nineteenth-century man was no real explanation. When he returned to La Scala in 1906 he performed Wagner and Verdi and other Italian operas. He conducted *Carmen* and *Louise* – but also Gluck's *Orfeo* and Debussy's *Pelléas*.

A caricature by the celebrated tenor Enrico Caruso who performed under Toscanini's baton at La Scala, Milan, in Buenos Aires and at the New York Metropolitan.

He supervised every detail of the production of *Pelléas* and in Gatti-Casazza's words 'transfused his entire being' to the singers. Even the stage-hands worked in stockinged feet so as not to disturb this new, subtle and restrained world of sound. Although there was worry enough about the audience reaction Toscanini hoped that Debussy would be present. He did not manage it, and in view of the cat-calls and general rowdiness Toscanini must have been relieved, even though the evening ended in success with him applauding the more intelligent section that remained. All the same, when he heard a French production of the work in Paris two years later he was appalled and told Debussy he now wished he *had* been at La Scala. The composer never heard him conduct *Pelléas:* when he next performed it at La Scala, in French and not Italian, Debussy had been dead for seven years.

The 1908 *Pelléas* was followed by Boito's *Mefistofele* with Chaliapin, who had sung in it with Toscanini in an earlier season and found him 'a man who really knew his job, and one who would brook no contradiction.' Toscanini had however allowed him certain freedoms, as was his way with artists he really admired. Another singer who had worked with Toscanini in Italy and South America was Enrico Caruso, but here the admiration was for the voice *as* a voice. Unlike Chaliapin he argued with Toscanini over his demand for full voice at rehearsal and he took increasing liberties in performance. When he held a high note far beyond its time Toscanini shouted at him in public 'have you finished, Caruso?' – but that was at the New York Metropolitan. Early in 1908 it was announced that both Toscanini and Gatti-Casazza would be leaving La Scala for the Met later that year. Caruso, who was already singing there, was one of several singers who heard the news with misgivings. The easy life had gone! The Met had wanted Toscanini for five years but fear of the unknown had held him back. When they also began angling for a new general manager and approached Gatti-Casazza, Toscanini decided that if Gatti went he would go as well.

Chapter Two

THE YEARS AT THE MET

So began Toscanini's long association with New York, first with the Metropolitan and at a later stage with the Philharmonic-Symphony and the NBC orchestras. As usual Milan greeted news of his departure with dismay and New York awaited his arrival with apprehension. There was however trouble before he left La Scala over a concert programme in which he had been asked to include a work by Gaetano Coronaro who had recently died. He would not be dictated to over programmes, and when another conductor was invited to take over, Toscanini brought an unsuccessful lawsuit. Milan heard him again as an occasional visitor, but it was not until after the war that he resumed his directorship of La Scala. Meanwhile his arrival at the Met with Gatti-Casazza in the autumn of 1908 caused some alarm in the company. In his book *The Maestro* Howard Taubman summed up the situation:[3]

> There were some singers who honoured Toscanini for his insistence on musical rectitude and for his unsparing efforts to build fine performances. But make no mistake about it, there were others who resented him as long as they were in the same theatre. There was a time early in Toscanini's stay at the Metropolitan when a group of principal singers signed a petition to the board demanding that Andreas Dippel, who was a co-manager of the company in Gatti's first two years, be retained. This was an open attack on Gatti, but the target was certainly Toscanini as much as, if not more than, Gatti.

Caruso, who was one of the signatories, was not the only singer to prefer a less strenuous existence even if it meant working at less than his potential. What a sacrifice! Toscanini's first opera at the Met was *Aida*, and Richard Aldrich wrote in the *New York Times* of his inspiring effect on the entire cast. 'Caruso' he said 'sang with probably more power . . . with a more prodigal expenditure of his resources than he has achieved before.' It was the same with the others whether they liked it or not: Emmy Destinn as Aida 'was fired with the prevailing spirit and let the audience hear the utmost sonorities of which she was capable.' Far from inhibiting his singers Toscanini's passion for 'musical rectitude' led them to surpass themselves. The orchestra too, according to Aldrich, had seldom sounded so rich and full or revealed so many finer details of the score. Toscanini was 'a man of potent authority, a musician of infinite resource.'

Toscanini with his daughter Wanda.

He had won over the orchestra at his very first rehearsal, which was not of *Aida* but of *Götterdämmerung*. His ear and his memory detected numerous misprints that had gone unnoticed by other conductors *with* the score, just as was to happen with *Tristan* at Bayreuth in 1930. At the Met however it had been assumed that he would concentrate on the Italian repertory and leave Wagner to Gustav Mahler, who had conducted *Tristan* there the previous season with Fremstad as Isolde. Although Mahler later told Bruno Walter that Toscanini performed it 'in a manner entirely different from ours but magnificently in his way' Aldrich's notice of Mahler's *Tristan* suggested certain common ideals:[4]

> His tempi were frequently somewhat more rapid than we have lately been accustomed to. . . . and yet the score was revealed in all its complex beauty, with its strands of interwoven melody always clearly disposed and united with an exquisite sense of proportion and an unerring sense of the larger values.

It is not true that Toscanini wrested the *Tristan* production from Mahler, though Alma Mahler made a point of this in her biography. He actually heard Mahler conduct it and found it the work of a tired man 'with no passion in it', though this was a later performance than the one Aldrich reviewed. When he eventually took over *Tristan* in his second season W J Henderson of *The Sun* expressed surprise at Toscanini's subdued treatment of the first act and at the electrifying effect this had on the later outpouring of passion, which was nevertheless unleashed 'with never a step beyond the limits of musical beauty'. This unique gift of seeing a large-scale work as a single entity was of course noted on many occasions. Mahler however did moderate his praise, according to Alma, with the expected reservation that Toscanini's *Tristan* was too Italian; yet years later Siegfried Wagner told Kipnis that the work ought to be sung *like* an Italian opera.

So where are we? No other Italian conducted Wagner, or anything else, quite like Toscanini – and in Italy he had been accused of Wagnerising Verdi! In New York the general pattern of criticism was of amazement and gratitude for the raised standard of music-making, whether the opera was German, Italian, *Carmen* or *Boris*. There was constant talk of vitality, dramatic force, musical beauty, of singers and orchestra being inspired, and of audience reaction to the music itself. Toscanini was, as Aldrich said, 'a strenuous force, a dominating power'. When he turned from the normal repertory to Gluck's *Orfeo* in that second season his direction was 'another manifestation of his versatility and power to identify himself with the spirit of different men, different periods and styles.' Knowledge and care alone do not make for such identification without the 'wholehearted devotion' that irradiated and unified the performance. This devotion, as at La Scala, was sure to lead to trouble with singers who chopped and changed, whether Caruso, Emma Eames or Geraldine Farrar. When Farrar reminded Toscanini that she was a 'star' he is said to have replied that 'the stars are in heaven – here we are all artists, good or bad.' Other singers of the Met years, like Louise Homer and Frieda Hempel, accepted the Toscanini discipline as a rewarding manifestation of his devotion. On the subject of discipline Giulini told Harvey Sachs that 'Toscanini fought terrible battles in order to achieve things which everyone today takes for granted', though the battles might involve volleys of Italian invective that even his admiring orchestra found hard to take at first.

There is no place here to list all the operas that were the beneficiaries. Rehearsals he naturally demanded, but he could also work miracles in an emergency. Within a few days of his New York début he conducted *Rigoletto* and *Tosca* for Francesco Spetrino, who was ill. He had no rehearsal for *Tosca* apart from a brief discussion with the singers but apparently transformed the work completely. Nor were his energies confined to the seasons at the Met. In the summer of 1909 he returned to Italy, conducting concerts including new works like Debussy's *La Mer,* and in 1910 he took the singers from the Met for an Italian season in Paris. There he performed *Manon Lescaut* and in such a way that the amazed Puccini asked him to edit a new publication of the opera. It was fourteen years since he had given the première of *La Bohème,* and in his next New York season he was to introduce Puccini's latest opera, based on Belasco's *The Girl of the Golden West.* Later that season he gave the American première of *Ariane et Barbe-bleue* by Dukas. On the evening before the first rehearsal he invited Busoni to dinner. Like most fellow-musicians Busoni was impressed by Toscanini's intelligence and astounded at his memory. He told his wife that 'this does not impede his other faculties as is often the case with such abnormalities. . . . but such achievements must wear him out; he is a bundle of nerves.' Busoni was only a year older than Toscanini, who was still conducting thirty years after his death in 1924.

Toscanini continued to work on both sides of the Atlantic, conducting opera and the Verdi *Requiem* at Rome in 1911 and going back to Turin in the autumn for concerts during the International Exhibition. Other guest conductors included Elgar and Debussy, who were doubtless surprised to find the orchestra familiar with their styles – Elgar also conducted the Mozart G minor Symphony! – but at that time Toscanini had been having trouble with his eyes and told his old friend Depanis that he had no desire to look at new scores. He had taken a vacation in the Alps, recalling his earlier relaxation of mountaineering, but on returning to New York for his fourth season he undertook a busier schedule than ever, with two more new productions: *La Donne Curiose* by Wolf-Ferrari and Massenet's *Manon.* Wolf-Ferrari was yet another grateful composer who said he never knew 'what was in his opera' until he heard it under Toscanini, and much the same was said by Italo Montemezzi of his *L'Amore dei Tre Re* two years later. Meanwhile Toscanini and Gatti had been re-engaged in 1912 for a further three-year term at the Met.

That year Toscanini's 'vacation' consisted of a return to South America

OPERA NEWS

PUBLISHED BY THE METROPOLITAN OPERA GUILD, INC. • VOLUME 21 • NUMBER 20 • PRICE 20 CENTS

THE LIVING TOSCANINI

IN THIS ISSUE

LA BOHEME

MARCH 25, 1957

In 1910 Toscanini conducted the Metropolitan première of *La Fanciulla del West* in the presence of Puccini. This well-known photograph of the conductor and the composer was taken by Lionel Mapleson.

where he conducted a colossal repertory of fifteen operas, including *Tristan* and *Götterdämmerung*, at the new and magnificent Teatro Colón in Buenos Aires. Back at the Met his next season introduced *Boris Godunov* to America. Chaliapin, an ideal Boris who had sung with him at La Scala in *Mefistofele*, could not be persuaded to go to New York at the time, and the title-role was taken by Adamo Didur, who as Aldrich reported achieved the finest success of his American career under the inspiration of 'the master hand'. Up to that time New York had heard Toscanini in five seasons of opera and in the Verdi *Requiem*. On 13 April 1913 he appeared there for the first time as a symphonic conductor in a programme consisting of Wagner's *Faust Overture*, Strauss's *Till Eulenspiegel*, and Beethoven's Ninth Symphony. The public interest was enormous, with thousands turned away, yet the *Herald* stated that it was 'a distinctly musical gathering'. There was an aura about a Toscanini concert that attracted musicians as well as laymen, even those who hoped to find something at which to carp. How would he deal with the Ninth, for example? His reading was not however that of an Italian, the *Herald* continued, but of 'a master of all schools'. Once again a sweeping statement? Aldrich's remarks in the *New York Times* are worth quoting at some length, and on the Wagner and Strauss too: [5]

> He revealed in the fullest measure the qualities of the great symphonic conductor . . . The *Faust* overture has seldom been made more impressive in its gloom and pessimistic spirit. The *Till Eulenspiegel* has seldom been played with a more dazzling brilliancy, verve and bravura, with a more perfect ensemble or a more complete mastery of all its bristling difficulties.
> . . . attention was naturally centred chiefly upon Mr Toscanini's performance of Beethoven's Ninth Symphony. . . . In this Mr Toscanini met in an unusual degree Wagner's criterion of the *melos*, of keeping unbroken the essentially melodic line that underlies it. The orchestra sang throughout; and in all the nuances of his performance the melodic line was not interrupted; nor, in all the plastic shaping of phrase was the symmetry of the larger proportions of the organic unity of the whole lost sight of. It was rhythmically of extraordinary vitality. It was a conservative reading without exaggeration or excesses. . . . It was devoted to the exposition of Beethoven and not of Mr Toscanini. . . .

The finale, Aldrich went on, was 'supremely stirring', the chorus 'sang with thrilling vigour', and the solo quartet mastered its difficulties 'with the appearance of ease'. Toscanini recalled that the quartet was the best he ever had for the Ninth: Frieda Hempel, Louise Homer, Carl Jörn and Putnam Griswold, all members of the company. There were reservations that 'some may have preferred the adagio a little slower' and a mild complaint that he made a break between this movement and the clamorous opening of the finale. Beethoven did not, by the way, write *attacca* at this point though many have felt a dramatic interruption implied. The other argument, borne out by the recitatives that follow, is that the clamour is directed not against the slow movement in particular but *all* the previous music – and that some separation is called for.

With the cast of the production of Verdi's *Falstaff* given at Busseto in 1913.

Since 1913 was the centenary of Verdi's birth, Toscanini's return to Italy took him to Busseto, the town near the composer's birthplace, where he conducted *Traviata* and *Falstaff* in the small theatre with hand-picked singers and players, as though the operas were chamber music – what one would give to have heard those! Then, in deference to the Verdi year, he gave some performances of *Falstaff* and the *Requiem* at La Scala, where the enthusiasm may be imagined. He had hoped to conduct Boito's long-delayed *Nerone* on that visit – with Caruso – but the scoring of the work was still proceeding laboriously and the composer never lived to hear its eventual première eleven years later. Boito was however overwhelmed, as in former years, by the 'immense intellectual joy' that the *Falstaff* performances had given him.

When Toscanini returned to New York for his sixth season at the Met, rumours began to spread about his unrest. He continued to work as strenuously as ever, making a great success of new operas like Montemezzi's *L'Amore dei Tre Re* and breathing new life into established ones like Verdi's *Ballo*. To the outsider his situation may have seemed secure, ideal and

33

triumphant. He had excellent singers, a good orchestra and a rapturous public. He could dictate his own terms – up to a point. There were of course inevitably a few who resented his discipline and his demands: musicians whose peace he disrupted and a small minority of critics who, like Ricordi in Milan, could not share his view that an opera should be as integrated as a quartet or a symphony. Tributes however continued to pour in during the following season – 1914 to 15 – when his productions of *Euryanthe* and *Trovatore* were among many to be seen and heard and revalued. An accusation that he kept all the best operas for himself was patently untrue: could his associate conductor Giorgio Polacco have made such a success of Montemezzi or Giordano? The fact remained that Toscanini was able to put across works where others failed. Polacco was given plenty of best-sellers, like *Aida* and *Tosca,* to conduct. Compare the situation at Barcelona in 1890 when a much younger Toscanini was himself an assistant and was detailed to take over Bellini's *Capuleti e Montecchi* at short notice. He did so to such effect that the chief conductor, Mascheroni, was furiously jealous and had the opera withdrawn.

Toscanini was disillusioned with the Met for more deep-rooted reasons than petty jealousies. His idealism, some would say his egotism and intolerance, caused growing conflicts. Both Gatti-Casazza and Otto Kahn, chairman of the directors, had a mundane attitude to finance and to the purpose of a great opera-house. As long as star singers filled the house and benefactors kept the books out of the red they were satisfied. Finance and

Gatti-Casazza, David Belasco, Toscanini and Puccini.

diplomacy were their prime considerations and Toscanini was interested in neither. When it was hinted that it would be diplomatic for him to conduct an American opera, Walter Damrosch's *Cyrano*, his thinly veiled excuse 'I do not understand English' hardly disguised his distaste for the work. On the other hand he became enraged when economies were made in rehearsals of repertory operas. There was a disastrous occasion in April 1915 when he conducted *Carmen*, with Martinelli and Farrar: the performance was fraught with mishaps, and to make matters worse Tullio Serafin, who was then chief conductor of La Scala, was in the audience. So this is what the much-vaunted Met can do! Toscanini conducted Mascagni's *Iris* the following night, cancelled his part in the rest of the season, and left the Met for good. Kahn and Gatti did their best to make him change his mind. He wavered a little, but it was too late. Once again there was a general chorus of despair. Whatever headaches he may have given people when he was in charge his loss was irremediable. Even Martinelli, the Don José in that last unfortunate *Carmen*, said 'he was the heart and soul of the Metropolitan'.

It is now clear, according to Harvey Sachs, that there was another and more personal reason for Toscanini's departure from New York: his affair with Geraldine Farrar, 'who told him that if he loved her, he must leave his family for her.' This he would never have done, but if that painful episode precipitated his return to Italy it brought with it an ironic stroke of good fortune. He had otherwise planned to sail on the last fatal voyage of the *Lusitania*.

Turin, 1911. Standing behind Toscanini is his wife: to his right, their daughter Wally.

35

Chapter Three

RETURN TO LA SCALA

Nothing apparently could induce Toscanini to go back to the Metropolitan, but in wartime Italy he threw himself into music-making as a free-lance. He gave benefit concerts and, in the autumn of 1915, undertook an opera season in Milan – not at La Scala, but at the Teatro dal Verme where he had conducted the première of *Pagliacci* twenty-three years before. This he revived in a repertory of half-a-dozen Italian operas including *Traviata* and *Falstaff.* Caruso, on vacation from the Met, sang in *Pagliacci*, and in *Traviata* the Violetta was Rosina Storchio, which must have been a traumatic experience for Toscanini, coming so soon after the Farrar episode. (The tragedy of the Storchio affair continued: their son, palsied and speechless, was to die three years later at the age of sixteen.) A season devoted to Italian opera in wartime was appropriate enough and there was never a doubt about Toscanini's intense patriotism. The prestige he had given to Italian music in general had been immeasurable, but he still held to his principle that art knows no frontiers. This ran him into serious trouble the following year when he conducted the first of a projected series of concerts at the Augusteum in Rome. Having begun with Corelli, Martucci and Tommasini he was about to continue with two Wagner extracts, but anti-German feeling was running high and the opening of the *Götterdämmerung* Funeral Music was greeted with the shout: 'For the dead in Padua!' The concert was abandoned in the general uproar and so was the rest of the series. Toscanini, who refused any payment for these wartime enterprises, made no more public appearances for a while. In 1917 however he made his own contribution to the war effort by forming a military band and conducting it at the front during the Monte Santo offensive, for which he was decorated for bravery under fire.

The Italian defeat depressed Toscanini profoundly, though early in 1918 he agreed to conduct some concerts at the Milan Conservatory to help the perilous state of many of the country's musicians. He played no Wagner but included the *Eroica*, which drew forth anti-German protests as well as praise, and some Russian and French works that were new to him, such as the Franck Symphony and Debussy's *Iberia*. Two composers for whom Toscanini had a special devotion were to die that year: one was Debussy, the other Boito. Boito's *Nerone*, on which he had worked for fifty years, was still incomplete, and as the war in Europe drew to an end Toscanini paid tribute to his friend and champion by conducting the much earlier *Mefistofele* at La Scala. There

Toscanini rehearses a military band at Quisca in 1917.

were some concerts in Turin and Milan including performances of Beethoven's Ninth but on the whole the period was marked by a running down of activity and a general pessimism. It was about this time too that he made a short-lived and unsuccessful foray into politics. With his despairing view of the future he had put his trust in the aspirations and promises of a young journalist called Benito Mussolini. He was even persuaded to offer his name as a candidate but the affair came to nothing and within a year or two his disillusionment with Mussolini was complete. The Fascist movement, as it became, was to be a thorn in his flesh for the next two decades and more.

Plans were meanwhile afoot to reform La Scala on an autonomous basis with support from public and private funds and local taxes. Toscanini had been approached and had stated his terms, which amounted to complete artistic authority over the venture. He knew enough about the ins and outs of opera-houses to accept nothing less, and sufficient about practical and mechanical details to advise and delegate. While the building itself was undergoing the needed refurbishments and improvements he formed a new orchestra of the best available players and took it on one of the longest and most arduous tours ever undertaken by a new organisation under a single direction. After two months' intensive rehearsing they gave thirty-three concerts in Italy in just over five weeks and then departed for North America. Toscanini spoke of his pride in the orchestra and its 'really perfect discipline' though on its first New York appearance Richard Aldrich expressed some disappointment:[6]

It is true that the Metropolitan Opera House does not yield the best acoustical results to orchestras playing on its stage . . . But other orchestras in the same position have sounded better than this one last evening. The strings seemed to lack not only brilliancy but amplitude and solidity. Nor were there unusual excellences at once apparent in most of the woodwind and brass, though there were passages in which they did themselves credit.

He wrote of the expected tumult of welcome that greeted Toscanini himself, but his strictures covered most of the performances. It is understandable that the acoustics could rob *Iberia* and *The Fountains of Rome* of colour and atmosphere, but Aldrich's remarks on Beethoven's Fifth are surprising in view of his almost unqualified praise of the Ninth in the same venue seven years before: [7]

> He employed no little freedom of tempo, in the first movement especially; but the tempo was in part of a deliberateness that seemed alien to the character of the music; a tempo that weighed uncomfortably upon the effect.

It is any way refreshing to find Toscanini criticised for excessive freedom – it was usually the reverse! – and those who heard him conduct the Fifth in later years will know that he allowed more room than most for the phrasing of the second subject and compensated by pressing forward urgently in the coda of the first movement. Fritz Kreisler, who heard him during that Scala tour, was so convinced that he said he would rather hear the Fifth 'wrongly played by Toscanini than correctly by anyone else.' Once again, who shall arbitrate between wrong and correct? From all accounts he was one of the first to take the opening bars up to tempo and not at a portentous and melodramatic half-speed.

The finale of the Fifth Symphony was one of several movements and short works that Toscanini recorded at Camden, New Jersey during the tour. The old acoustical process was primitive and exasperated him. He demanded retake after retake, nearly ruined the company's finances, and called the results 'a real pile of rubbish'. With a skeleton of an orchestra playing quiet passages *forte* in order to get them on the wax the records are hardly a reliable guide, but their origin and vitality are unmistakable. Robert Marsh, in his analysis of the Toscanini recordings, gleaned enough to make some valid comparisons with his later interpretations, noting that his way with Italian music changed less than with the German classics, but this first experience was unfortunately to give Toscanini a distaste for recording for many years.

The American visit, which also took in Toronto and Montreal and involved sixty-eight concerts in just over three months, was a marathon in itself but was followed by further extensive touring in Italy. All this meant that when La Scala re-opened at the end of 1921 Toscanini had a well-seasoned orchestra at his disposal, brought up on a wide range of concert works and styles, and well aware of his ideals and methods. The autonomous Scala was more democratic than the old, with new restrictions on box-holders and the like, and Toscanini chose to inaugurate it with Verdi's *Falstaff,* in which

Mariano Stabile sang the part with him for the first time. He favoured singers for their patience and adaptability as much as for their voices: another was Toti dal Monte, his Gilda in *Rigoletto,* and he repeatedly re-engaged the tenor Aureliano Pertile who took over Faust in *Mefistofele* at short notice. The first season also included *Boris* and it ended by restoring the Verdi-Wagner balance with *Meistersinger,* though Verdi, as Harvey Sachs has described it, had replaced Wagner as the house-god in the new establishment.

Klemperer, who was then in charge of the opera at Cologne, heard the *Meistersinger* production the following year and later wrote in a Berlin weekly about the unforgettable impression and about Toscanini in general:[8]

> If one can separate legitimate and illegitimate art phenomena, then Toscanini is legitimacy personified; he is the king of conductors. His performances are more than beautiful, they are right. Toscanini is the ideal representative of objectivity. It would be difficult to point out anything peculiar in his interpretations; that is the peculiarity of his method of making music. In 1923 I heard a *Meistersinger* performance under his direction at the Scala in Milan, and I can say nothing about it but that I have never heard a similarly perfect musical presentation of the work in any theatre in the world.

Klemperer was to tone down such unqualified praise of Toscanini in later years, especially and expectedly over matters of tempo, but coming at that time from a leading German conductor his words were unbelievably impressive. They echoed the sentiments that had already been expressed during the Scala Orchestra's American tour by such diverse musicians as Monteux, Bloch, Kreisler and Paderewski. Did not Paderewski write that 'he is a transcendent genius – a genius of the first order'?

Ironically enough the new Scala and its transcendent genius, which had quickly become once again the pride of musical Italy, were already coming to blows with the Fascists, who had seized power shortly before the second season opened. Toscanini's attitude to Mussolini, in whom he had put some faith at the end of the war, had changed completely, like Beethoven's to Napoleon at the time of the *Eroica.* In fact Toscanini's incomparably resolute conducting of the *Eroica,* whatever its original intention or dedication, always seemed to express a universal call to freedom. When rehearsing the first movement with the BBC Orchestra in 1937 he told them: 'Is not Napoleon, is not Hitler, is not Mussolini – is Allegro con brio!' It was however a very different piece of music that came to be associated with Toscanini's defiance of Mussolini: the notorious Fascist anthem *Giovinezza.*

The first showdown came during a performance of *Falstaff* in the second Scala season. Some Fascists demanded the anthem and in spite of demonstrations and disruptions Toscanini refused – as he always did. Similar incidents occurred during the next few years, culminating in the drastic Bologna affair of 1931. *Giovinezza* was to become the symbol of Toscanini's hatred for Mussolini, like a nightmarish but unplayed rondo-theme.

41

Another rondo-theme, always returning in different guises, was that of the relationship with Puccini. Puccini had been all for Toscanini at their first meetings over *La Bohème* in 1896 but thereafter his attitude changed like the weather. They argued violently over politics before the 1914 war – Puccini was pro-German at the time – and when Puccini heard that Toscanini had criticised his *Trittico* operas adversely he wrote him off with contempt, one would have thought for good. The revival of *Manon Lescaut* at La Scala in December 1922 brought them together again. As of old, Puccini found Toscanini 'a real miracle of feeling, of refinement, of sensitivity, of balance.' In reply to suggestions that he touched up the scoring of the opera this was denied in a letter to the *Corriere della sera*. Puccini had in fact done 'some substantial retouching' but he underplayed this in order to give all the praise where he felt it belonged:[9]

> My *Manon* is exactly that of thirty years ago, only it has been directed by Arturo Toscanini, which means directed in a way that brings its composer the great and rare joy of seeing his music illuminated with the same brightness that he saw and dreamt at the moment of composing it and never saw thereafter. . . . No, it is simply itself, enlivened by the greatest animator the art of music can boast of.

Puccini wrote and told Toscanini that he had given him the greatest satisfaction of his life. Was this really the man who had said 'I won't have this *God*, he is no use to me' four years before? There were obviously difficult temperaments at work on both sides. Only a few months before their reconciliation Puccini could still write: 'There's a thorn in my side: that Toscanini, who persists in his enmity to me!'

Toscanini's next important assignment for Puccini was to be a sad one: the posthumous production of *Turandot*, which he left unfinished on his death in 1924. Franco Alfano, a prolific composer in his own right and professor of composition at Turin, was invited to complete the closing scene and though Toscanini kept a watchful eye on the proceedings he was unhappy about the result. The first performance, in 1926, was in any case purposely and dramatically cut short as Puccini had left it, with Toscanini's moving words, variously reported, about the master laying down his pen. Even that occasion was haunted by the ghost of *Giovinezza*, since Mussolini wished to attend. It became a test-case of *Giovinezza* or Toscanini and by a series of tactical moves Toscanini won an outright victory over the Duce by keeping him out of the theatre.

Mussolini had also taken a personal interest – at a distance: he was not in Milan – in the success of another 'unfinished' opera, Boito's *Nerone*, which Toscanini had at long last put on in 1924. Boito had died six years before and his admiration for Toscanini, unlike Puccini's, had been steadfast and unchequered. *Nerone*, as has been said, occupied him for half-a-century and the scoring was still incomplete when he died in 1918. Toscanini called in

Vincenzo Tommasini to help in the gargantuan task of putting it all together from Boito's copious annotations. A great fuss was made over the première, which was an overwhelming success, but it is worth noting that when Toscanini left La Scala it dropped from the repertory. Only he, it seems, had the gift, the love and the patience to make the massive whole convincing. He included extracts from *Nerone* in a Boito programme at La Scala many years later – in 1948, the thirtieth anniversary of Boito's death – but it was the Prologue from *Mefistofele* that brought down the house.

Toscanini's battles with the Fascists over *Giovinezza* became an annual event on Empire Day, when its playing was obligatory. One move was to close the theatre and arrange for rehearsals on that day. Other incidents gave Toscanini chances of venting his wrath, including the tragic case of Giuseppe Gallignani, the director of the Milan Conservatory, who committed suicide after being dismissed from his post without warning. Filippo Sacchi described the dramatic scene at the funeral over the hypocritical 'tributes':[10]

> When the coffin was lifted into the hearse it was followed by an enormous wreath with gold lettering on the ribbons: 'From the Minister of Public Education'. Toscanini shouldered his way through the crowd, shouting in a voice hoarse with fury: 'Take that wreath away at once!' He then seized it himself and flung it into the road with all his might. Nobody in the procession dared to touch the crushed and soiled wreath, and it was left lying on the roadway.

He also snatched and trampled on the papers of a would-be speech-maker who had instigated a campaign of slander against Gallignani.

Such events, as well as increasing taunts and decrees from the Fascists, added to Toscanini's unrest. Once more the irony was at work. He had left La Scala in 1908 under a cloud and the New York Metropolitan in 1915 under another. New York had always wanted him back, as it showed vociferously on his tour with the Scala Orchestra, and moves were quickly made to invite him as a guest of the Philharmonic. The Chicago Opera also wanted him but (as usually happened when he was not interested) they received no reply to their invitation. In any case he was pledged to La Scala, where he had an absolute control unobtainable elsewhere. The young conductor Gianandrea Gavazzeni witnessed the results and told Harvey Sachs fifty years later how Toscanini had instituted 'a custom, a method – a tyranny, one could say'. He went on:[11]

> La Scala was completely reorganised for Toscanini, in respect to its rehearsal habits, to the way of conceiving its programme, to the method of making singers study, and also in respect to educating the public. The public with Toscanini, during that era, was educated to consider the theatre not as something for amusement, but as something with a moral and aesthetic function, which enters into the life of a society, into the life of a culture.

Of course Siegfried Wagner had remarked on the excellent discipline at La Scala, including the intelligent audience reaction, when he heard *Tristan* there during Toscanini's much earlier tenure. The Scala of the nineteen-twenties far surpassed it, from all accounts. Things were not always perfect – how could they have been? – and when mistakes occurred Toscanini was the first to suffer. Antonino Votto, one of his assistants, reported a case when Toscanini himself made a bad slip during the dress rehearsal of Pizzetti's *Dèbora e Jaéle*. He was so shocked that he cancelled the rest of the rehearsal. These were exceptions, of course, and Puccini summed up Toscanini's achievement when he wrote that 'he has created an institution which is the pride of Italian art.'

After four seasons, faced with growing harassment from Mussolini, he at last accepted an invitation to appear as a guest with the New York Philharmonic, and on 14 January 1926 he appeared with it for the first time. Nineteen years later, almost to the day, he returned to the orchestra – then the Philharmonic-Symphony – and conducted the same programme: Haydn's 'Clock' Symphony, Respighi's *Pines of Rome*, Sibelius's *Swan of Tuonela*, Siegfried's Death and Funeral Music from *Götterdämmerung*, and Weber's *Euryanthe* Overture. A recording exists of the 1945 concert and the playing is superb, although Toscanini had not been the regular conductor of the

Toscanini with his wife and daughter, Wally, after a gala performance of *Die Meistersinger* at La Scala, Milan, to Mark the 30th anniversary of his association with the world-famous opera house.

44

With Zoltan Kodály in the gardens of the Villa d'Este on the shores of Lake Como, 1928.

orchestra for over eight years. All his unique qualities of balance, ensemble, attack and precision returned to them in an instant. He had been pleased enough with the orchestra in 1926 to return to New York the following two years, causing some apprehension with his Scala colleagues and increasing discomfort to Mengelberg and Furtwängler, who were also conducting the Philharmonic. He had met Furtwängler when he came to direct some concerts at La Scala and their relations had been cordial enough, but direct rivalry as guests in New York was another matter. Furtwängler, who was jealous by nature, obviously resented Toscanini's enormous public success, and so did Mengelberg, the orchestra's regular conductor, though it was he who had made some of the approaches to get him in the first place. Having got him, New York was certainly determined not to let him go. When he eventually left La Scala for good to take up the principal conductorship of the Philharmonic, Toscanini invited Mengelberg to continue as a guest though the latter can have had little cause for comfort. Toscanini had a far greater admiration for Furtwängler, whom he suggested as his successor when he retired from the Philharmonic in 1936, though Furtwängler did not take it up, largely due to American anti-Nazi feeling at the time.

Toscanini's busy seasons at La Scala were naturally better organised than they had been at the Metropolitan, where he once conducted three different operas, one of them *Tristan*, within two days, but they were hectic enough. Harvey Sachs noted that he led fifty-one performances of fifteen operas during the 1925-6 season in spite of spending the month of January with the New York Philharmonic. He also conducted orchestral concerts in Milan from time to time, took the Scala orchestra to Turin and Switzerland, and in 1927 celebrated the Beethoven centenary with complete cycles of the symphonies in both Milan and Turin. That year he produced *Fidelio* for the first time. Other important productions of those years included Debussy's *Pelléas*, now done in French, in 1925, and his first complete one of *Parsifal* in 1928. He had been furious at the indifferent reception when he had given extracts from it at La Scala twenty-five years before, but the public now received it well, having grown to accept the Wagnerian time-scale under Toscanini's incomparable direction in *Tristan* and *Meistersinger*. Mozart, on the other hand, was a stumbling-block. In 1923 Toscanini produced *The Magic Flute*, which was coolly received. Mozart, even the Italian operas, did not go down well in Italy in those days and, as we know, Toscanini had a life-long Mozart problem. *The Magic Flute* he loved, and he opened the next season with it as well, as though to pay the audience back for its indifference. In 1929 he prepared *Don Giovanni*, which he had not produced since his Buenos Aires season of 1906. He cancelled it during rehearsals. The indisposition of the Don Ottavio and his dissatisfaction with the Donna Anna were given as excuses, but Sachs perhaps rightly suggests that Toscanini's doubts about his own understanding of the Mozartian style may have been the true reason.

46

Toscanini's last opera that season, which turned out to be his unannounced farewell, was appropriately enough the one that had launched his career: *Aida.* Immediately afterwards he took the Scala company on tour to Vienna and Berlin. The impact in both places was phenomenal. The press bandied words and phrases around like 'absolute perfection', 'ecstasy', 'delirious enthusiasm', 'stupefying' and so forth, and musicians were equally stunned. In Vienna the young Herbert von Karajan recalled being 'completely disconcerted by the perfection' of *Falstaff. Lucia,* too, of which he had previously thought 'What can there be in this?', astounded him by its 'infinite significance'. In fact the world of Italian opera, including such well-worn repertory pieces as *Trovatore* and *Rigoletto,* was suddenly seen in a completely new and elevated light by the German-speaking public. Many of us have had the uncanny experience of hearing a familiar work from Toscanini as though for the first time, even without the inestimable added bonus of the corporate spirit and discipline that he had instilled into La Scala for almost a decade. Yet the greatest moment of triumph marked the end of that association. No sooner was the tour over than his retirement was announced. 'He will give up operatic conducting' stated the *Berliner Tagblatt.* This was not quite true, of course. Siegfried Wagner had been at the Scala's Berlin performances and at long last decided to invite him to Bayreuth the following summer. The glories of the Salzburg Festivals were to come later on in the nineteen-thirties. Meanwhile the New York Philharmonic-Symphony awaited him. He had spent the earlier part of 1929 with them, approving the higher standard of playing after the merger of the two orchestras (hence the new title) and making some recordings, including the well-known ones of the 'Clock' and the 'Haffner'. In October he opened his first season as principal conductor. As in 1908, when he left Milan for the Metropolitan, La Scala was shocked. Its standards soon declined. An article in the *Frankfurter Zeitung* had summed it up during the visit to Germany: 'Toscanini is not La Scala: one can imagine him even without it; but La Scala today is a collective Toscanini. It is his will and his work.'

BAYREUTH AND SALZBURG

The outstanding qualities of the New York Philharmonic-Symphony at the time can be judged from the records Toscanini made with it in early and late 1929. The 'Clock' and 'Haffner' symphonies and a handful of shorter works were soon looked up to as 'classic' interpretations, though the 'Haffner' in particular may surprise later listeners with its freedom of tempo in the opening bars and the trio of the minuet. He regrettably made no further records for seven years, but in 1930 he took the orchestra on a European tour that is still talked about by older generations. He then went to Bayreuth to conduct *Tannhäuser* and *Tristan*. Yet, apart from the rift with Mussolini, his explicit reason for leaving La Scala had been the need for a less turbulent life! The strain of running an opera-house to his own standards was severe enough

The New York Philharmonic Symphony Orchestra with Toscanini on their European tour in 1930.

even without political harassment, and quite a different matter from conducting short seasons as a guest. His New York visits had also made him dissatisfied with the orchestra at La Scala, in spite of the miracles he is said to have achieved with it, and Bayreuth was to provide a far greater let-down. American standards were high – think of Boston and Philadelphia – and the combination of New York and Toscanini phenomenal, as Europe was soon to learn.

It was barely a year since the triumphant visits with the Scala company to Vienna and Berlin. Having shown how Italian opera really could sound, Toscanini now demonstrated his powers as a symphonic conductor. He had of course conducted a vast amount of orchestral music since his early days in Turin, but his main centres of activity had always been opera-houses. When he left La Scala for good in 1929 the change of emphasis was clear and was somehow epitomised in those two tours. The tour with the Philharmonic-Symphony was an extended one, taking in fifteen cities within a month and a day. Everywhere the reaction was of stunned amazement, but in Italy the admiration must have been tempered with an acute sense of personal loss. Toscanini did not conduct in Italy again for sixteen years, though in 1931 he prepared two concerts of Martucci's music at Bologna that never took place, thanks to *Giovinezza* and the Fascists. The New York tour began in Paris and ended in London, and the impact of Toscanini's first visit to England is described elsewhere. At one of the Paris concerts there was an incident with Ravel, who complained that his *Bolero* was played too fast, but the paper *Excelsior* reported: [12]

> Here, truly, is a master, not only a conductor, but a master of all conductors. . . . He was able to achieve a precision of execution from his orchestra which, for us, has something of the inexplicable and wondrous about it: it is absolute, unarguable and overwhelming material perfection.

Praise like this followed Toscanini and the orchestra throughout the tour and within a few weeks he was to miss his 'faithful friends' of the Philharmonic-Symphony and of whom he was so proud. When he heard the orchestra at Bayreuth he walked out of the first rehearsal in shock and disgust.

The shock may well have been great, for the Bayreuth orchestra was a largely *ad hoc* affair drawn from various parts of Germany for the duration of the Festival. Rudolf Schwarz, who was then conductor at the opera in Karlsruhe, told me how casual the preparations had been, and how he suddenly found himself playing the triangle in the hastily improvised percussion section at the end of Act 1 of *Tristan*. There was an expected blow-up when Toscanini began the *Tannhäuser* Overture and could not get the players to take the important triplet-figure in tempo, so deeply ingrained was the laborious German manner of sitting heavily upon it. Further trouble followed with the crescendo, or lack of it, at the start of the second act, but although Toscanini went nearly berserk in his cries of 'crescendo,

Bruno Walter, Toscanini, Erich Kleiber, Otto Klemperer and Wilhelm Furtwängler in Berlin, 1930.

cre-scen-do!' he never for one moment lost control of the ensemble. Everyone, as usual, was amazed at his memory and his ear. In *Tristan* it must have been humiliating for the established Wagnerites, conductors like Karl Muck and Siegfried Wagner, to find how many misprints had gone undetected for half-a-century. Even over production details Toscanini was secure in his knowledge. Bayreuth had introduced a gradual light-change between the Venusberg and Wartburg scenes in *Tannhäuser* and Toscanini insisted on a sudden one. Research proved him right: he knew more about Wagner's wishes than the initiates.

Yet the idea of an Italian presiding at the Wagnerian shrine had appalled the establishment and especially Karl Muck, who had conducted *Parsifal* there as long ago as 1901 and was to do so again in 1930. Muck must also have been aware of the effect it might have on his own prestige, since Toscanini's immense services to Wagner over the years were common knowledge. Siegfried Wagner, on the other hand, had wanted Toscanini at Bayreuth for a long time, though by a tragic coincidence he died of a heart attack while that 1930 Festival was in progress. A memorial concert was given at which both Toscanini and Karl Muck conducted, and the singer Alexander Kipnis compared their contributions: [13]

> On the programme was the *Siegfried Idyll* conducted by Toscanini: it was the most beautiful *Siegfried Idyll* I have ever heard in my life; and everyone

in the audience had tears in his eyes from the sound of this music, and the thought that the Siegfried for whom it was written was no more. Then old Muck conducted the Funeral March from *Die Götterdämmerung*: it was so old, like a piece of parchment, a piece of dusty old scenery – in comparison with the unbelievably beautiful *Siegfried Idyll.*

One should not however discredit Karl Muck's long reputation as a Wagner authority. There were some no doubt who found Toscanini's Wagner too clear, too clean, too Classical, too Italian in fact, though on the question of style Siegfried Wagner had made his remark to Kipnis, before Toscanini came to Bayreuth, that *Tristan* should be sung *like* an Italian opera. Ernest Newman wrote about this in an article called 'Music and Frontiers':[14]

> If a conductor is a man of supreme genius he will vivify the music he takes in hand whatever be its country of origin or his own birthplace. . . . Toscanini's *Meistersinger* and *Tristan,* whether they speak to a German listener with the authentic accent of Berlin or Dresden or not, are unsurpassed in my experience for depth of feeling and beauty and clarity of texture.

I wrote to thank Newman for expressing this so well, and he replied by recalling his impressions of that 1930 *Tristan,* twenty years after the event: 'In some inexplicable way one heard *everything* in the complex texture without feeling that anything in particular was being stressed for "bringing out" sake. I still feel baffled when I think of it.' He soon wrote again going into more detail, mentioning in particular the unbearable poignancy of the dot-and-slur figure in the cellos as Isolde sings 'von seinem Lager blickt' er her' in her Narration in Act 1: 'it was heart-breaking; the whole of the sick Tristan's suffering was in it.' This little two-note figure is quite subsidiary and usually goes unnoticed, but it is the only part in the texture to carry the marking *sehr zart* (very tenderly). Yet Toscanini did not 'bring it out': there was no *insistence* upon it, said Newman, but 'soft as the cello tone was, it filled the whole theatre'. This uncanny quality of projection was also mentioned by the critic Ferruccio Bonavia over a similar incident in the third act, about which everyone asked afterwards 'what has he done with it?'. He had done no more, of course, than observe and realise the beauty of something that was there already.

Toscanini also conducted *Tannhäuser* in 1930, which was perhaps even more of a revelation in view of the tendency of most people to patronise the work as 'early' Wagner. Newman recalled this in *The Listener:*[15]

> What made my experience with *Tannhäuser* so extraordinary on that day in 1930 was the feeling that any such well-meant adjustment of the critical faculty was unnecessary. . . . I had the curious sensation that the gap of the years had in some mysterious fashion narrowed, and that I was listening to *Tannhäuser* very much as the first audiences, and indeed the composer himself, must have listened to it in 1845 – to a new work intensely serious in purpose and palpitatingly alive, an operatic organism of a new order.

Toscanini in Bayreuth, 1930.

It is of course easy enough to point out harmonic banalities and commonplace sequences in the light of *Tristan* or *The Ring*, but Toscanini had a miraculous way of elevating such things. Having heard him conduct only the Overture and Venusberg Music in the concert-hall, in London in 1937 and Lucerne in 1946, I was astounded at the absolute nobility of music in which no commonplace existed. That old war-horse, the Overture, was suddenly invested with a supreme dignity and, as might have been expected from him, countless surprises of detail. For those who have scores, the noble effect of the major key in bar 31 after the pathos of bar 23 was just one such detail. What

Bruno Walter, Thomas Mann and Toscanini in Salzburg.

had he done? As with the *Tristan* example Newman quoted, it was hard to say; yet the music sounded so different, so infinitely natural and expressive.

The tragedy is that Toscanini was not in charge when Columbia made records of that 1930 production of *Tannhäuser*. Apart from his general antipathy to recording there were problems over his long-term contract with Victor in America. Karl Elmendorff conducted instead, though the strong influence of Toscanini has been remarked upon by those who attended the Festival. A similar effect of lingering fire was often noted when other conductors took works over from him. The BBC Orchestra's performances of Brahms's Fourth in 1935 and Beethoven's *Eroica* in 1937 at the London Proms under Sir Henry Wood were remarkable cases of this. Toscanini's visits earlier in those summers had left their mark, and Sir Henry must have been well aware of this.

In 1931 Toscanini returned to Bayreuth to conduct *Tannhäuser* and *Parsifal*. Contrary to his later reputation for taking some works on the fast side it is worth noting that his timing of 5 hours and 5 minutes for the actual music of *Parsifal* was by far the slowest ever recorded in the Bayreuth archives. Even Knappertsbusch's more recent and much-praised reading, which was on the most spacious lines, took twenty-five minutes less. Although Toscanini undoubtedly speeded up some works in his later years the stop-watch often had surprises in store: a steady but firmly-held rhythm can convey far more vitality than a scrambled one, and in slow-moving music, like much of *Parsifal*, he never lost the sense of a continuous unbroken line. He regarded these visits to Bayreuth as a kind of sacred duty, the apotheosis of his love for Wagner's music, and he refused any fee for them. This did not prevent him from speaking his mind, throwing tantrums if necessary, and expressing his growing disillusionment with the internal politics of the Festival. *Parsifal* was in any case a special labour of love for him. It was thirty-two years since he had made his own pilgrimage to Bayreuth to hear the work he came to consider as the most sublime of all the music-dramas. The conductor Basil Cameron spoke to me of the magnificence of that 1931 *Parsifal*, especially of the Grail scenes, though Toscanini was suffering from severe pain in his right shoulder that summer. A few weeks before, in May, had come the Bologna incident.

His New York winter seasons were busy enough with the Philharmonic-Symphony, and Toscanini's pattern of spending the summer months in Europe was familiar enough from his old days at the Metropolitan, except when he varied it by taking on extra seasons in Buenos Aires and Montevideo. Europe was to see and hear plenty of Toscanini during the nineteen-thirties though his activities were to be constantly dogged by the march of Fascism. In May 1931, shortly before his second visit to Bayreuth, he had gladly offered his services to conduct two concerts at Bologna in memory of his old friend Martucci. They were to be devoted entirely to Martucci's music, but the Fascists demanded *Giovinezza* as well and Toscanini was beaten up by hooligans as he arrived at the hall. Needless to say the concerts were cancelled and Toscanini, his passport removed and his house under surveillance, became world news for his resolute stand against Mussolini. As for the Duce, his initial feelings of elation at having scored a point against this troublesome musician soon faded under the pressure of outside opinion. Toscanini was eventually allowed to leave, but though he continued to visit and stay in Italy until shortly before the war he never conducted there again until his triumphant return to La Scala in 1946.

Meanwhile the German scene was changing rapidly and in the same direction. At Bayreuth Toscanini was alarmed to find Siegfried Wagner's widow, Winifred, a strong supporter of Hitler and the up-and-coming Nazi party, but in the end he agreed to return in two years' time for the next Festival and to conduct *Meistersinger*, a work he loved dearly and for which he had done so much. By 1933, however, the Nazis had taken over and Toscanini's name headed the list of eminent musicians who protested against the boycotting of their Jewish colleagues under the new régime. It soon became obvious that he would not return to Bayreuth under such conditions, just as it was obvious that Bayreuth needed him for its own standards and prestige. A personal request from Hitler, which he acknowledged politely, did not make him change his mind. Germany's loss was soon to be Austria's gain – until Hitler intervened there too.

After the Bayreuth cancellation, moves were made for him to make some

In rehearsal with Lotte Lehmann, Salzburg 1934.

guest appearances with the Vienna Philharmonic, first through Hugo Burghauser, the orchestra's president, and later through the violinist Bronislaw Huberman. In the autumn of 1933 he conducted the Philharmonic in Vienna for the first time and in programmes largely devoted to its own classics. Burghauser, who was also first bassoon of the orchestra, spoke of the reaction of the players: [16]

> The orchestra, which had been day in, day out with Strauss, Weingartner, Bruno Walter, and by then also Klemperer, with this ensemble of the greatest talent of the world – the orchestra, with Toscanini, realised this was the climax of every musician's experience. Not only because he was superior to other conductors – which was taken for granted; but because he made us *superior to ourselves* – which was the phenomenon that was practically unexplainable.

He added that familiar works like the Beethoven Seventh, which they all knew in their sleep, were 'as newly created for us'. In fact the Viennese, renowned for their conservatism, were as overwhelmed by Toscanini as Bayreuth had been. He in turn was impressed enough with the qualities of the Philharmonic to agree to return the following year and to give some concerts at Salzburg as well. His singer in a Wagner programme was to be Lotte Lehmann, whom he had heard in Strauss's *Arabella* while in Vienna and engaged to sing with him that winter in New York. Lehmann was to figure importantly when Toscanini conducted opera again in the next three

Toscanini rehearsing *Fidelio* with Lotte Lehmann in Salzburg in 1935 and (*right*) in conversation with Madame Thode, Cosima Wagner's daughter, at Bayreuth.

Salzburg festivals from 1935 onwards. She now regretted that she had fought shy of him and declined an invitation to sing at La Scala in the nineteen-twenties. The musical recompense was well worth, as she dramatically described it, the 'perpetual shaking and quaking in anguish and pain' of rehearsing with him. Not all his rehearsals were like that anyway. When she first sang to him he was so mild and friendly that her fears vanished, but she soon learnt how he suffered when his demands for absolute precision and complete spiritual surrender were not met.

It was during his return visit to Vienna in the autumn of 1934 that Toscanini conducted the Verdi *Requiem* as a memorial tribute to the Austrian Chancellor Dollfuss, who had been assassinated in a Nazi plot that summer. The wisdom of this gesture has been queried in view of Dollfuss's own dictatorial methods and his alliance with Mussolini, but it was primarily an anti-Nazi move. German music-lovers and Nazi officialdom also took note of Toscanini's growing allegiance to Salzburg and when it was announced that he would conduct *Fidelio* there in 1935, within a few miles of the German border, its message of heroism triumphing over tyranny had clear implications. He also made Verdi's *Falstaff* a condition of his acceptance. There were inevitably other conductors who feared or resented Toscanini's successes, and this time it was Clemens Krauss, director of the Vienna State

Opera, who planned to forestall this *Falstaff* with a German production of his own. Bruno Walter on the other hand, who welcomed Toscanini with open arms both as an artist and for his defiance of the Nazis, had some doubts about the suitability of Verdi's late masterpiece for a festival so deeply imbued with the spirit of Mozart.

In the end Toscanini won, of course, and *Falstaff* become one of the main attractions of all three of his Salzburg opera seasons. Mariano Stabile, who had sung the part many times with Toscanini at La Scala, was the Falstaff, and assisting at rehearsals was the young Erich Leinsdorf, who described that first 1935 performance as 'of unmatchable perfection'. Felix Weingartner, who did not even mention Toscanini's name in his autobiography *Buffets and Rewards,* told the Vienna Philharmonic, which always played for the festivals, that he had never dreamt of such perfection, and Karajan had said much the same when Toscanini, with some of the same singers, had taken *Falstaff* to Vienna with the Scala company six years before. Salzburg however had the Philharmonic's own superfine qualities to contribute. The Vienna strings played with the unity and precision of a quartet, and the vocal ensembles were performed with a breath-taking finesse that only Toscanini, it seemed, could achieve with such apparent spontaneity.

In *Fidelio* Toscanini surprised the purists by making a musical concession to Lotte Lehmann, who was singing Leonore. He greatly admired her artistry but knew of her increasing problems in taking the vital top B at the end of her aria. In view of the opera's carefully planned key-scheme it may seem amazing that he should agree to transpose it down a semitone from E to E flat, thereby destroying the effect of E major as symbolic of freedom. This 'pragmatic' solution, as Leinsdorf called it, was effected by replacing E minor harmony with C minor at the word 'nieder' three bars before the key-change preceding the aria itself. (Kipnis, who sang Rocco in the 1937 revival, told of a touchingly amusing sequel: that when rehearsing the grave-digging duet in Act 2 Toscanini was so overcome by the music that Lehmann went to him and kissed him. 'If you do that again' he said 'I will not transpose your aria!') Toscanini's complete absorption with *Fidelio* affected everyone, and even such details as the unanimity of the wind-chords that accompany Leonore's 'Ich habe Mut!' in the first-act trio resound in the memory of those who heard it. There was criticism here and there of Toscanini's tempi – Furtwängler, one read, told him that the Prisoners' Chorus was too fast! – but Arnold Rosé, who led the Philharmonic and was then in his seventies, said it was the first time he had played *Fidelio* at the *right* speeds. Once again, who shall arbitrate here? Any departure from tradition was sure to be attributed to the fact that Toscanini was Italian, and when he added *Meistersinger* to his Salzburg operas in 1936 and 1937 there were a few patronising remarks about *I Maestri Cantori.*

The general impression at Salzburg was of the unique vitality and clarity and the unifying influence that Toscanini brought to everything he

Toscanini with Bruno Walter and Stefan Zweig.

undertook, and since the events were broadcast they could be shared with listeners all over Europe. Two chance overhearings, picked up from foreign wave-lengths in the summer of 1936, made me determined to get to Salzburg the following year. One was of the electrifying effect of the crescendo leading to the recapitulation in *Leonore no 3*, with its staggered rising dissonances, played as only the Vienna strings with Toscanini could play it. (Toscanini kept to the now discredited tradition of playing the overture between the two scenes of Act 2 of *Fidelio*.) The other unforgettable impression was of the beauty of the rise-and-fall in the extension of the Prize Song in *Meistersinger* just before Eva's 'Keiner wie du'. In both cases the particular eloquence was unmistakable. On this subject of eloquence and beauty in music Georg Tintner, a conductor I greatly admire, recalled the extraordinary effect Toscanini achieved earlier in Act 3 of *Meistersinger*, when Beckmesser staggers into Sachs's empty room nursing his beatings of the previous night. The music is humorously grotesque and Toscanini read it as such, but his ear for balance made it an episode of beauty also, an observation that could have applied to the texture of the whole of those Salzburg performances.

Since I attended the 1937 Festival I also have vivid recollections of many such details. Was it Italian and therefore not *echt* to reveal the contrapuntal lines of the score so firmly but tenderly as in the first-act gathering of the masters, or to show that sentences may form paragraphs and paragraphs chapters? In any case Wagner was the beneficiary, which takes one back to Newman's remarks about Toscanini at Bayreuth. The London *Times* commented on the 'not very distinguished singing', and one missed Lotte Lehmann and Charles Kullman who had sung Eva and Walther the previous year. Once again the real revelations were in the shaping of the whole and the miraculous texture: [17]

> The famous beauty-spots – for instance, the aftermath of the riot in Act 2 and the end of Sachs's 'Wahn' monologue – seemed more beautiful than ever, not cheating expectation. But the merit of this performance was that the same glamour was given to passages which are too often dry and uninteresting as music. The accompaniment to Beckmesser's serenade, played with an astonishing appearance of freedom and spontaneity yet with every note in fact precisely graded in dynamic relation to the next, was but one of these passages. . . . the intellectual concentration that could control the whole of this vast score down to the last demisemiquaver is something beyond one's experience. Need it be added that it was Signor Toscanini who stood at the conductor's desk?

The most controversial of Toscanini's Salzburg operas was *Die Zauberflöte*, which he added to the repertory in 1937. Kipnis, who sang Sarastro, found most of the tempi too fast but some, like his own 'O Isis und Osiris', uncomfortably slow. The contrast between solemnity and comedy was in fact strongly drawn, and it was remarked ironically that the whole was worth hearing for the sake of the C minor duet of the armed men in the finale of the second act. Was the general problem the eternal one of style – that the very positiveness of Toscanini's approach, some would say his god-like masculinity, precluded the pathos of the shadows, even the frailty, for want of a better word, that was paradoxically Mozart's greatest strength? Spike Hughes, one of the many Toscanini admirers to have grave reservations about his Mozart conducting, found much to praise in the opera but quoted the postlude to Pamina's G minor aria as an example of a failure to perceive the emotion behind the notes. If this amounted to the defect of a virtue, an abhorrence of sentimentality, I noted as an anomaly that *Falstaff*, along with its scintillating wit, had yielded a tenderness of a Mozartian kind in the music of Nannetta and elsewhere. Toscanini's performances of Mozart operas had been few enough in half-a-century and he never directed another. Bruno Walter, who conducted *Figaro* during the 1937 Festival, congratulated him after *Die Zauberflöte* but Toscanini told him frankly: 'You cannot like it; you were trained on the slower German tempi.'

Toscanini still made occasional visits to Vienna itself and also took the Philharmonic to Budapest and Prague. He admired the music of Kodály and

Toscanini with Rachmaninoff in Switzerland.

played his *Psalmus Hungaricus,* and in turn Kodály dedicated one of his last works, the Symphony in C, to his memory. There were also orchestral and choral concerts during the Salzburg festivals, including the Brahms and Verdi Requiems. The Salzburg operas were performed in the Festspielhaus, a rectangular building with poor stage facilities and limited accommodation. Plans for improvement were put into action and Toscanini had agreed to include *Tannhäuser* in the 1938 season, but hopes were dashed when Hitler walked into Austria the following spring. Toscanini's fruitful collaboration with the Vienna Philharmonic had ended, and except for a staged programme of Boito extracts at La Scala after the war he never conducted opera in the theatre again. Instead he took part in summer festivals at Lucerne until the war put a stop to these too.

In 1950 he was invited back to Vienna to conduct the *St Matthew Passion* during the Bach Festival. He declined, and how he might have interpreted a work of which he had only previously performed the final chorus is a fascinating conjecture. Karajan conducted it instead, and according to Howard Taubman the involvement of Karajan and Furtwängler in the post-war Salzburg festivals ruled out any possibility of his return. Memories of Hitler's Germany and those who had worked within it were still too vivid. He did not however allow such feelings to cloud his musical judgment. In 1950 he attended Karajan's performances of the Bach B minor Mass and Beethoven's *Missa Solemnis* at La Scala, and made a point of sending a message of thanks to Furtwängler after a broadcast of Berlioz's *Faust.*

★　　★　　★　　★　　★

It seems appropriate to add a note here about some of Toscanini's other European activities during the nineteen-thirties. He paid several visits to Paris to conduct the Walther Straram Orchestra. He had shown a special understanding of Debussy ever since his first *Pelléas* at La Scala, and *La Mer* became one of his most famous interpretations. Although he incurred Ravel's displeasure over the *Bolero,* Ravel did not deny his fantastic gifts – 'he is, all

Toscanini with Bronislaw Huberman and members of The Palestine Symphony Orchestra (now The Israel Philharmonic Orchestra) in December, 1936.

the same, a great virtuoso' – and wanted him to conduct his Left Hand Concerto with Wittgenstein, though this never transpired. According to Marguerite Long, Ravel also heard and admired his performance of the *Daphnis and Chloe* second suite, though he would not go to see him afterwards. Paris and London were not the only European capitals to welcome him as a guest. He also visited Stockholm and The Hague. In many ways the most significant gesture was proposed to him by Huberman, who had also been a prime mover in getting him to conduct the Vienna Philharmonic. With Jewish musicians turned out of their posts by the Fascists and many of them fleeing from Europe the idea of the Palestine Orchestra arose. Toscanini was the ideal person to launch it and he emphasised his willingness by declining any fee or expenses for his visits. He conducted several concerts in Tel-Aviv, Jerusalem and elsewhere, took the orchestra to Cairo and Alexandria, and returned the following season in the spring of 1938. On this second visit he insisted on including some Wagner – the *Lohengrin* preludes – which had been banned for understandable reasons that Toscanini would not accept. Great art, he maintained, transcends politics. It was a battle he had fought before and he won his concession as a matter of principle.

Meanwhile Toscanini's visits to England had become eagerly awaited annual events. His concerts were confined to London – and Oxford, where he took the BBC Orchestra in June 1937 and gave his services in aid of the University's Foundation Fund. It was typical of him to refuse the honorary doctorate that had been offered him, and just as typical that he should give them a richly generous programme in return, including Beethoven's *Pastoral* Symphony, Brahms's First, and the Haydn 'Oxford' Symphony, which he prepared specially for the occasion. His effect on the London scene, however, obviously calls for a fresh chapter.

Chapter Five

TOSCANINI IN LONDON

Considering the tumultuous welcome that always greeted Toscanini in Britain it is surprising and rather sad to reflect that he never conducted in London until he was sixty-three. The occasion was the triumphal tour in 1930 with the New York Philharmonic-Symphony. There had been many moves to get him before. The London Symphony Orchestra, which he never conducted, had had him high on its list of desired guests ever since its founding in 1904. Paris, after all, had heard him in an opera season as early as 1910 and it could have been argued that both North and South America had had more than a fair share of his gifts. Toscanini never alas conducted opera in England, though there had been talk of his coming to Covent Garden in 1919 for the European première of Puccini's three one-act operas, *Il Trittico*. He openly expressed delight at the third of these operas, *Gianni Schicchi,* but his criticisms of the other two reached the ears of the composer, who declared 'I don't want that *pig.* . . . I won't have this *God.'* This did not prevent Puccini from eating his words later, when Toscanini revived *Manon Lescaut* at La Scala, and he died safe in the knowledge that his unfinished *Turandot* would be entrusted to his ideal interpreter.

Two other plans failed to materialise. Toscanini was actually engaged for a Royal Philharmonic Society concert in February 1923 but called it off through ill-health, aggravated no doubt by his strenuous activities at La Scala that season. A visit with the Scala Orchestra itself had also been hoped for, and Sir Adrian Boult recalled the tactics of the enterprising but disappointed impresario:[18]

> He poured out a marvellous series of stories of Toscanini's 'temperament' for the benefit of the more sensational gossip columns. It is natural that one who is endowed with such tremendous vitality and magnetism should have a strong temperament, but nothing I have ever heard or seen of the Maestro and his work is out of line with a perfectly consistent pursuit of the ideal in music and an absolute horror of personal publicity and showmanship.

This last impression was in fact the overriding one when Toscanini eventually arrived in London at the end of his European tour with the New York players. He gave four concerts, two in the Royal Albert Hall and two in the Queen's Hall. Cynics could say that the thought 'Toscanini at last!' would have been enough to stir up a gullible public regardless of the actual performances, but what of the really discriminating listeners who flocked to the concerts, the respected colleagues and the hard-to-please critics? Everyone, it seems, was bowled over by the virtuosity of the playing. Yet, a familiar pattern by now, there was no doubt about the absolute subservience of this to a purely musical purpose.

'There is in Toscanini's conducting no trace whatever of display or showmanship or self-consciousness', wrote W J Turner. Sir George Henschel, the first-ever conductor of the Boston Symphony and in his youth a friend of Brahms, was full of praise for Toscanini's reading of Brahms's Second Symphony. He also told his daughter Helen: 'I never expected to hear the *Eroica* played like that this side of Heaven!' Toscanini also included a work by the London-born Eugene Goossens, who had incidentally deputised for him on his non-appearance seven years before. In his autobiography *Overture and Beginners* he wrote of the occasion in some detail: [19]

> The *maestro* again included my *Sinfonietta* in one of his programmes and played it miraculously. I went round to thank him after the concert, but this being his first experience of the Albert Hall and its then appalling acoustics, the great man was inconsolable and near to tears at what he considered fine performances ruined by the triple echo of the hall. I tried to explain that many seats in the hall were immune to this echo, but he refused to be comforted and repeated: *'Non, non, non; orribile, brutto, spaventevole, acusticamente ridicolo'* and further choice expletives. At Queen's Hall he was happier, but complained, *'Molto risonante, ma troppo piccola per un gran' orchestra.'* Toscanini and the superb orchestra swept London like a fire, and furnished for some years a standard of performance which, alas! judging by present-day English playing, is but a vague memory of the past.

Goossens was admittedly writing some twenty years after the event when domestic standards were only beginning to recover from the disruptions of the Hitler war. The point must be made again that it was not simply the superb orchestra, but the superb orchestra under Toscanini's direction, that created the lasting sensation. The desire to hear him again with or without the Philharmonic-Symphony was paramount. Meanwhile one of his interpretations, that of Elgar's *Enigma* Variations, aroused some adverse criticism: undeniably brilliant, but was it *English* enough? This question was to be answered and in Toscanini's favour by two acknowledged Elgarians when he played the work in London again five years later.

The first concert had been attended by the King and Queen and Toscanini raised no problems over playing national anthems on tour as a matter of courtesy – and *how* he played them! The Fascist *Giovinezza* in Italy was another matter. In London nine years later there were however raised eyebrows and rude comments when he declined to be presented to royalty during the interval of the first of his Beethoven series with the BBC. On that occasion the playing of *God save the King* had been resplendent, with Toscanini facing the royal couple as they took their seats in Queen's Hall; but during the concert itself a still higher rule, of absolute concentration on the music, prevailed. If Toscanini's refusal was considered an insult one might well have asked what the audience, all of it, had come for in the first place.

This 1930 New York visit certainly stirred up dissatisfaction with the regular London orchestral scene, and it is fair to add that Furtwängler's concerts with the Berlin Philharmonic also shook British complacency. Two new developments were to enliven the situation, however: in the autumn of 1930 the recently-formed BBC Symphony Orchestra began its first season of public concerts with Boult as chief conductor; and in 1932 Beecham, not to be outdone, founded the London Philharmonic. Beecham's LPO was to play regularly for the Royal Philharmonic Society and for the Royal Opera's summer seasons at Covent Garden. The BBC, apart from its studio commitments, provided Sir Henry Wood with a good permanent orchestra for the continuation of the Queen's Hall Proms. It soon began to welcome important guest conductors such as Koussevitsky and Bruno Walter. Recordings by Boult, Elgar and others added to the orchestra's prestige. In 1933 Koussevitsky's performance of the Sibelius Seventh Symphony was taken 'live' from the Queen's Hall and issued by the Sibelius Society, and the following year some much-praised recordings with Bruno Walter included Brahms's Fourth. When Toscanini's son-in-law Horowitz played the Tchaikowsky B flat minor with Boult he no doubt reported on the orchestra's quality. British music-lovers were also getting to know Toscanini's art through the records *he* had made in 1929 with the Philharmonic-Symphony in New York.

To bridge the gap between the winter seasons and the Proms the BBC instituted a London Music Festival in the early summer. Koussevitsky took part in 1933 and again in 1935, but although he was a 'star' conductor and famous for his work with the Boston Symphony his eloquence was marred for some listeners by his expressive liberties. Barbirolli wrote about this at the time and made an interesting comparison: [20]

> I do feel that his attitude of not disciplining himself at all in regard to matters of style, and in giving the impression that he must 'interpret' everything before the music can come to life, is not in the highest ideals of our art. Perhaps the simplest way to put it is that his attitude is the direct *opposite* of Toscanini. The latter radiates something very *pure* and *noble* whereas I cannot help sensing some of the showman in K.

Koussevitsky fans might take the reverse view that it is the performer's prerogative to indulge the spirit, however personal, at the expense of the letter of the score; but his strange vagaries of tempo were duly noted in the records he made with the LPO of the Mozart G minor and the *Eroica*. He also conducted the *Eroica* with the BBC during the 1935 Festival when his three

With his wife on a shopping expedition in London, 1937.

concerts were to be followed by four from Toscanini. This was Toscanini's second visit to London and his first appearance with a British orchestra. Players said that Koussevitsky had warned them: 'You may think *I* am difficult, but just you wait!' Boult later told a very different story: 'Needless to say, the orchestra worshipped the Maestro from the first rehearsal. . . . Alas, one person was not amused: Koussevitsky.'

Toscanini, having won over and amused the players with his remark 'just an honest musician', had begun his first rehearsal by playing straight through the middle movements of the Brahms Fourth. Boult recalled that the Toscanini hallmarks were immediately apparent, such was his power of communication. The BBC may not have matched the Philharmonic-Symphony in precision and virtuosity but, as Boult had shown himself, it had its own qualities: a warm sonority in the strings, some outstanding wind-players, and the quick adaptability that has so often impressed guest conductors of British orchestra in general. But from this moment, since all four concerts were broadcast, personal memories crowd in vividly. There had been some complaints about the BBC's policy of selling tickets in advance of the programme details, but after the event the editor of *Rimington's Review,* a record magazine, went overboard in the opposite direction though only about Toscanini: 'He alone of all performers is welcome whatever he conducts.' Such a sweeping remark was sure to come under fire, but the alchemy had worked again, and Toscanini's 'unenterprising' programmes had at least opened with a comparative rarity, the overture to Cherubini's *Anacreon.*

The performance of the Brahms Fourth that followed was bound to evoke comparisons with Bruno Walter's recent recording with the same orchestra. Walter had taken a legitimate, warm-hearted and relaxed view of the work – some may have preferred it – and it is sufficient to say that with Toscanini a different orchestra and a different work emerged. My still vivid impression is of a nobly austere and tragic intensity, a sense of inevitable unfolding of a musical argument, together with an uncanny transparency of texture. A later London critic wrote of Toscanini's predilection for a 'saturated sound' and this was true of the unbelievable richness at the return of the second theme in the slow movement. Richness maybe, but without a trace of sentimentality, though for radio listeners a ghost voice, somewhere between singing and humming, appeared to be shaping the long melodic line. Toscanini's own *cantabile,* audible on some of his records, never disturbed those in the hall, and in future seasons the BBC kept its microphones at a safer distance. When the Brahms was repeated in Toscanini's second concert *The Times* wrote: 'Herein the performance is a 100 per cent solution of the music, the "how" and the "what" are made one, and the absorption of the listener in the nature of the thing so created is whole and complete.' This, I felt, did not rule out other valid interpretations of the work but testified to Toscanini's intense conviction, command and sense of structure.

Part two of the first concert (3 June 1935) had been devoted to the Funeral

Music from *Götterdämmerung*, so magnificently conceived that it silenced any complaints about Wagner extracts, and Elgar's *Enigma*, which brought some of the usual reservations about style. Three days later a letter appeared in *The Times* from Sir Landon Ronald, a notable English conductor and friend of the composer, who went to extremes in his defence of Toscanini and declared that 'this great conductor rendered the work exactly as Elgar intended'. Yet Boult, also renowned as an Elgar interpreter, rushed to second Ronald's remarks and carried them still further: [21]

> An artist of the calibre of Toscanini seems to have the power of grasping the essence of the style of any music he touches, and it has been a great experience for all of us to hear him unfolding the beauties of everything he has rehearsed with us, always in what seems to be inevitably the right musical language.

There were of course countless details in Toscanini's *Enigma* that came as surprises, but who shall say that Elgar did not *intend* them since they were part of the score? In turn Toscanini was surprised at the British laxity over a work he had introduced to Italy thirty years before with only the printed notes to guide him. Bernard Shore, the principal viola, wrote of the immense care he took over the theme and its supporting harmonies. A notable break with tradition came at the return of the 'Nimrod' theme in the finale, where Toscanini took a broader tempo at the word *grandioso* and then led back to, but not beyond, the original speed. It is printed that way and the resultant apotheosis and continuity are thereby enhanced, though Elgar did not follow this himself. How could Toscanini have known this when he studied the work? On the vexed question of style Ernest Newman summed up the feelings of many, just as he had done over Toscanini's Wagner at Bayreuth: [22]

> When Toscanini conducted the 'Nimrod' of the Enigma Variations in London some of us may have been conscious of a slight non-English 'accent' in the music; but in spite of that the performance soared to a height and plumbed a depth I have never known it approach before or since.

The second 1935 concert had included more Wagner – the *Faust Overture* and the Prelude and Good Friday Music from *Parsifal* – and in the third and fourth the plan of repeating certain works meant that Debussy's *La Mer* and Beethoven's Seventh were heard twice. *La Mer* was a revelation for most of the players ('We didn't really know what it was about until *he* came') but the Beethoven raised some controversy over the trio of the scherzo, which Toscanini took at a quicker tempo than usual, thus flouting the dubious tradition of the Pilgrims' Hymn. In spite of the evidence of the score, in which Beethoven wrote *assai meno presto* and not, as is often heard, *andante sostenuto*, the laborious tradition still lingers. J A Westrup, however, chose the Seventh to epitomise his feelings about Toscanini's visit: [23]

To hear not merely this or that part, a salient melodic figure or a grinding bass, but every thread at once in the great texture of Beethoven's Seventh Symphony, must have stung even finished and finite clods to a recognition of genius. Seen thus, not darkly but face to face, music holds us as nothing else can. We can do anything but escape from it. It is a fortress of the spirit against a brutish, earthy world.

★   ★   ★   ★   ★

Boult spoke of the overwhelming reaction of the British public, but plans to invite him back in 1936 went adrift. In 1937 however Toscanini returned to take over the whole of the London Music Festival and, as expected, all six concerts were sold out within hours. This time the programmes and some of the performances came in for more widespread criticism. Toscanini could be praised for including a Cherubini symphony and excused for his enthusiasm over his compatriot Tommasini's *Carnival of Venice;* but it seemed perverse to follow the Mozart G minor Symphony with Bach-Respighi, and Debussy's *Iberia* with the Hungarian March from Berlioz's *Faust.* This kind of hotch-potch programme-building was of course common enough in older days, but it seemed a waste of Toscanini. I was lucky enough to attend all six concerts, which were my first experiences of him in the flesh. The excitement of this fact did not dull the critical faculty. In the opening concert there was an electrifying performance of Busoni's *Rondo Arlecchinesco* with Heddle Nash as the off-stage singer, but after the First Symphony of Brahms there was some awkward talk about style and fidelity.

Fidelity to the score had always been one of Toscanini's strongest principles, though he did not carry this into pedantry if he felt that minor adjustments would clarify the composer's apparent intention. In *La Mer,* for example, he reinforced the famous passage for divided cellos with violas and is said to have had Debussy's approval. He accepted some of the traditional extensions of the horn and trumpet parts in Beethoven which had been advocated as commonsense by Wagner and Weingartner. Attitudes have changed: nowadays even slight and rational alterations tend to be frowned upon as alien to the original style – or seen as the thin end of the wedge. But when Toscanini added some alien drumrolls to reinforce the return of the chorale-theme at the end of the Brahms First he created an anachronism that disturbed the purists. To report this may seem trivial in view of the general magnificence of the concerts but there were some other signs of disquiet among the critics. His reading of the Mozart G minor Symphony, always a controversial one, was considered dull by some on this occasion. At least two of the concerts were unforgettably wonderful: the Shostakovich no 1 and the *Eroica* on 4 June, and an all-Wagner programme on 16 June. During the war, when Toscanini's first NBC recording of the *Eroica* appeared, with its strangulated sound quality, I thought back (as I still do) to that memorable evening in the resonant acoustics of the old Queen's Hall.

70

Toscanini did however make quite a few records with the BBC Orchestra in the Queen's Hall and the first sessions took place when he returned later in 1937 to conduct two concerts in the orchestra's winter series. He recorded two works he was about to perform with it, Beethoven's First Symphony and Brahms's Tragic Overture, as well as the *Pastoral* which had been played earlier in the year. The first two were to be companions, as it were, for the forthcoming performances of Beethoven's Ninth and the Brahms *Requiem*. This was the first time Toscanini had conducted an English choir, the BBC Choral Society, and years later he spoke with admiration of its chorus-master Leslie Woodgate. The Ninth was of course eagerly awaited. Just before it began Helen Henschel, who was sitting behind me and had been at the rehearsals, whispered 'you have never heard anything like the first movement'. Toscanini's conception of this movement has caused some distress over the years through its urgency and forward drive that might seem to belie the marking *un poco maestoso*. Beethoven however had noted the word 'desperation' (Verzweiflung) in his sketches, and according to Sir George Smart had recommended an impossibly fast timing (forty-five minutes!) for the whole work. Furtwängler, also well-known to London audiences, had taken a totally different view of the first movement, allowing moments of mystery and reflection that were swept away in Toscanini's elemental drama. But when I took part in a broadcast discussion with several others about a dozen or so recordings of the Ninth, Toscanini and Furtwängler were the only survivors at the end of the debate.

In his book *The Orchestra Speaks,* Bernard Shore wrote in detail about Toscanini's rehearsing methods. I was present at many of the London rehearsals including one or two that Shore described, and witnessed both the infinite patience and the occasional explosions. Toscanini was sometimes criticised for demanding the ultimate from his players at rehearsal, just as he expected his operatic singers to use full voice; but for him the making of music called for complete involvement whether an audience was present or not. As a result some of the rehearsals were even more moving than the actual concerts because of the added intimacy and absence of distractions. There were times in fact when they amounted to performances, when he would play through whole works or movements with the minimum of comment. At other times he spent what seemed an eternity on some small detail, as happened with Debussy's *Iberia* in the 1937 series. His notorious rages, directed as much against himself as the players, were few and far between in the rehearsals I attended, but if the fear of them brought increased determination and concentration he can hardly be blamed for them. One thing seemed quite clear: that the unique Toscanini sound, the unique balance and ensemble, derived spontaneously from his gestures and the mind behind them rather than abnormal rehearsal time. This had been the secret of his first unrehearsed *Aida* in Rio. It was the 'miracle' that Klemperer and others could not explain.

Bernard Shore said that unlike many guest conductors Toscanini made no fuss about the seating of the orchestra. The one thing he was adamant about, the separation of first and second violins to his left and right, raised no problem since this was Boult's practice anyway. The musical reasons for this were shown clearly enough when Toscanini began his 1938 series with Mozart's *Magic Flute* overture, in which seconds are answered by firsts at the start of the allegro. There were again arguments about his too Beethovenish treatment of Mozart and about a programme in which the Weber-Berlioz *Invitation to the Dance* followed Vaughan Williams's *Tallis* Fantasia. The series was above all memorable for three things: Richard Strauss's *Don Quixote,* with Emmanuel Feuermann as the cellist; two performances of the Verdi *Requiem;* and, in the last of the six concerts, Sibelius's Second Symphony. At a rehearsal of the Verdi there was a blow-up with the soprano, Zinka Milanov, whom some of us recognised as the Zinka Kunz who had sung in the work with Toscanini the previous summer, but he continued to admire her voice and she returned to London for the Beethoven *Missa* in 1939. The overwhelming effect of the Verdi, which was preceded by the *Te Deum,* could have been foreseen and has already been mentioned. The Sibelius, on the other hand came like a bolt from the blue. Toscanini had already conducted *En Saga* with the BBC and admired the strings' handling of the long and difficult arpeggio passages. His ability to make an entire orchestra sound, sing, breathe and balance itself like a gifted soloist was never more impressive than in the great build-ups of the symphony. The audience's reaction obviously demanded his return for the sake of the music he played, and in 1939, under the gathering clouds of the Hitler war, he conducted all nine symphonies and other Beethoven works, including the *Missa Solemnis,* as part of a wider-ranging London Music Festival.

Toscanini's annual visits were awaited with excitement and a certain trepidation: how to get tickets? A ballot system had been introduced to reduce the black market, but the many disappointed applicants could at least hear the broadcasts. He had played all the Beethoven symphonies in his previous BBC seasons except the Second and Eighth, and he had told Sir Adrian Boult that he now wished, as it were, to put a seal on his visits with the complete cycle. For the middle three concerts of symphonies he put the even before the odd numbers, the Fourth before the *Eroica* and so on, and his companion works for the Ninth included the middle two movements of the op 135 Quartet. There were interpretative insights from which string quartets might learn, and there was historical interest in hearing this music in relation to the Ninth. But to play part of such a hallowed work on massed strings was a curious idea that annoyed many people, including those who accepted the *Grosse Fuge* in this way and even regarded Weingartner's orchestration of the 'Hammerklavier' Sonata as an 'interesting experiment'. Boult conducted the *Grosse Fuge* in one of his own concerts during the Festival, but even with Toscanini the BBC strings found it hard to cope with the scherzo of op 135 *en masse.* Toscanini often proved that he could make an orchestra play *like* a quartet, as in his NBC recording of these movements, but the result could not possibly *sound* like one. Adolf Busch, whose quartet played the late Beethoven works incomparably, never quite forgave him for his trespassings.

Meanwhile Toscanini visited Glyndebourne to hear Adolf's brother Fritz Busch conduct Verdi's *Macbeth.* If the war had not come, he might have been persuaded to do *Falstaff* there himself – he had declined the suggestion – since the idea of a small theatre for that most mercurial of operas had always attracted him. Significantly and movingly Toscanini's last London concerts in 1939 were devoted to performances of the *Missa Solemnis.* I attended both and also heard the last rehearsal, which had the complete sense of dedication of another performance. It had just begun when I arrived at the Queen's Hall. I heard the opening *Kyrie* through the closed doors of the Grand Circle which hardly impeded the projection of its warmth and sonority. Toscanini's sense of rhythm was as remarkable in slow-moving music as in the vivace of the *Gloria* that followed, and in the *Gloria* the most abrupt contrasts of mood and tone were achieved, as written, with no change of pace. In the *Credo* he reinforced the bassoon counterpoints – wrongly or rightly? – to clarify the problematic scoring at this point. Yet within the grandeur of the whole there were so many lovingly shaped details that one has never heard that way since, not even in Toscanini's much-later NBC recording. The *Qui Tollis* was one such episode, and the balance between choir and woodwind at *Qui propter nos homines* was another. Toscanini often brought the wind-players forward in sound but this alone could not explain the effect. The soloists – Milanov, Thorborg, von Pataky and Moscona – were hard put to it in the 'amen' section of the *Gloria,* where Toscanini read the *poco più allegro* as a stepping-stone to the *presto.* Those who could not face, or did not approve of, such a blazing intensity might look elsewhere for a more reflective view of the *Missa,* but the serenity of the *Benedictus* and the awe of the *Sanctus* were also unforgettable. As for the world outside, the final words 'dona pacem, pacem' seemed appallingly apt but in vain. It was Toscanini's farewell to the BBC Orchestra. London did not see him again for thirteen years.

After that 1939 rehearsal of the *Missa* I ran into Archie Camden, first bassoon of the BBC, and he was full of amazement at Toscanini's physical powers of endurance at the age of seventy-two. We little thought that fifteen years of such activity lay ahead, and when the war came most of his British admirers despaired of hearing him again in person. His NBC recordings, whatever their drawbacks, continued to reach Britain; and the BBC broadcast records of live performances given with the NBC, including a Brahms series. In November 1942 a concert of American music, with Earl Wild and Benny Goodman playing in *Rhapsody in Blue,* was relayed direct. After the fall of

Mussolini the following year Toscanini gave his services for the only film he ever made, and Londoners were able to see close-ups of him conducting Verdi's *Forza* overture and *Hymn of the Nations,* which he adapted to include the appropriate national anthems. One London musician was shocked that a great man should lend his art to jingoism, and the American censor completed the corollary by ludicrously cutting the 'Internationale' from this unique document when relations with Russia cooled after the war.

In 1946 Toscanini returned in triumph to La Scala and part of the opening concert in the rebuilt opera-house was relayed by the BBC. It was soon announced that he would bring the Scala Orchestra to Paris and London that summer. Since the Queen's Hall had been destroyed the London concert was to have taken place at Covent Garden, but Toscanini cancelled both visits at the last minute owing to an Allied decision to cede some Italian territory to France. It was a bitter disappointment, but Toscanini was obdurate and took the orchestra instead to neutral Switzerland where by pure chance I was able to hear his Beethoven-Wagner programme in Lucerne. I have written elsewhere about my pilgrimages to meet and hear him in Italy in 1949 and he seemed deeply touched that London should want him back so much. A year later he agreed to return to the BBC Symphony for the opening of the Royal Festival Hall in 1951. The news was greeted with great applause at the foundation-stone ceremony, though there were a few complaints in the press about the engagement of a *foreigner* for the inaugural concerts! Toscanini never came anyway: he had a knee injury and a minor stroke. All his summer arrangements in 1951 were cancelled, and London lost its only chance of hearing him conduct Vaughan Williams's Sixth Symphony, a work he never actually performed.

Toscanini's illness also forced him to sacrifice one of his dearest wishes: to conduct *Falstaff* again at Verdi's birthplace. He was eighty-four and hopes for a return to London faded rapidly. But in 1952 Walter Legge arranged a continental tour by the Philharmonia Orchestra under Karajan, and he persuaded Toscanini's daughter Wally to get her father to listen in to the Milan broadcast. He told Legge afterwards that he was neither too old nor too busy to conduct *his* orchestra, and the news soon spread like wildfire that he would give two Brahms concerts at the Festival Hall that autumn. Some of the Philharmonia's younger members were sceptical about all the fuss and excitement, but after the first rehearsal Frederick Thurston, who had also played the clarinet in Toscanini's BBC days, asked them 'didn't you know?' The concerts were not without incidents. Besides the four Brahms symphonies it was decided nearer the time to add the Tragic Overture to the first programme and the 'St Antoni' Variations to the second. As he was about to begin the first concert he was reminded to play the National Anthem, which he had not rehearsed but conducted with his usual dignity and grandeur. Whether or not this preoccupation was to blame, his next downbeat was for the First Symphony and the orchestra responded with the two sharp

Toscanini on his departure from London after giving two concerts in the Royal Festival Hall in 1952. With him is his granddaughter Emanuela Castelbarco.

chords of the Tragic Overture. The shock must have been paralysing, and although he recovered himself quickly the pacing of the overture had been taken from his hands and the somewhat hectic playing rubbed off on the symphony that followed. Too much was made over the fluffed trombone entry in the introduction to the finale – Toscanini blamed himself for his own loss of control – but an expected hero of the occasion was Dennis Brain, the first horn, who played his solos more marvellously than ever in both concerts.

The second concert was one of the most moving I ever experienced, and the final rehearsal equally so. At the rehearsal Toscanini simply played through the Brahms Third and Fourth symphonies without a break, except for one detail in the middle section of the passacaglia of the Fourth, and then spent the second half attending to the 'St Antoni' Variations in some detail. After the orchestra had played the difficult fifth variation particularly well he asked for a *bis* (encore) for his own pleasure. In the variation preceding, the rising and falling woodwind scales were so perfectly matched that an experienced orchestral player in that private audience exclaimed 'this is the master!' There was no personal hysteria about this – we all felt the same – and after the Third Symphony that evening Walter Legge was content to remark: 'To my present way of thinking, that is the greatest performance I have ever heard of anything.' The impression of having been at one with an ideal conception of the work's form and spirit was complete. Toscanini's NBC record of the work, pored over and tape-edited, was to bear no comparison with that live event in the Festival Hall. The Fourth Symphony, also magnificent, was interrupted by two deafening explosions during the passacaglia. Toscanini did not flinch for a moment, but the vandals who planted fire-crackers in the hall would have been lynched if the audience had got at them.

When Toscanini returned to New York he told the NBC players that the Philharmonia was one of the best-disciplined orchestras he had ever conducted. In his very last years he wanted to return to England – but it was too late. Neville Cardus, who had never been uncritical of Toscanini's uncompromising nature, had written of the autumnal beauty and valedictory sadness of that last Brahms concert, adding that 'it was not easy to look upon this wonderful old man without feelings not only of the highest esteem for his art, but also affection for him personally.'

THE NBC SYMPHONY

When Toscanini resigned from the New York Philharmonic-Symphony in 1936 he suggested that Furtwängler should be invited to succeed him. Although their musical approaches were usually held to be diametrically opposed Toscanini had a high regard for him and once said he considered his 'way' with Wagner just as valid as his own. There is little evidence that Furtwängler was as generous in return. According to Hans Keller he dismissed Toscanini as a mere 'time-beater' who relied on a motoric sense of rhythm as a substitute for the subtle and often extreme flexibility of pulse that characterised his own conducting. Toscanini's respect for Furtwängler fell away rapidly over his supposed capitulation to the Nazis, and when they met at Salzburg in 1937 Toscanini is said to have criticised his 'exaggerated and hysterical' performance of the Ninth Symphony as an expression of his moral weakness. Fritz Busch and Artur Rodzinski were also proposed by Toscanini for New York but in the event the Philharmonic-Symphony offered the post to Barbirolli. Although he had no real authority to choose his successor Toscanini was annoyed that he had not been consulted, though he later apologised to Barbirolli for behaving 'like a pig' over his appointment. Barbirolli may have been criticised in New York for not maintaining the unique Toscanini standard – who would not have been? – but he held the conductorship for six years, and for five of them, though it could hardly have been foreseen, he was to have direct competition from Toscanini himself.

As usual Toscanini's career was unpredictable. New York had certainly not seen the end of him as a symphonic conductor, but how would it get him back? In Europe Toscanini still lived in Italy though he refused to conduct either there or in Germany. He visited London, Paris, Stockholm and The Hague as a guest conductor and always with fantastic success. He had irked the Fascists by giving his services to the Palestine Orchestra and by drawing music-lovers from all nations to Salzburg. Storm-clouds were looming even though many refused to see them. The 1937 Salzburg Festival was Toscanini's last: in the following year, after the Anschluss, his *Meistersinger* production was taken over, ironically, by Furtwängler. There remained the Lucerne Festivals in neutral Switzerland. It is curious to imagine Toscanini's activity or non-activity in a Europe at war. He would certainly not have worked, even under threat, in a Fascist or Fascist-occupied country. He might have lived as an exile in Switzerland or come to England – or returned to

America. What would he have conducted and where? He often confessed himself tired out, but usually followed such assertions with an outburst of energy that would have floored men half his age. This had been his excuse for leaving La Scala in 1929 and one of his excuses for retiring from the Philharmonic-Symphony in 1936. Early the following year and within a few weeks of his seventieth birthday he was visited in Milan by Samuel Chotzinoff, who had been sent by David Sarnoff of the Radio Corporation of America to sound him about a new venture.

Chotzinoff elaborated on his mission in his book *Toscanini: An Intimate Portrait* nineteen years later, though his journalistic and anecdotal account is frowned upon by serious researchers. The main purpose was to persuade Toscanini to return to New York and take over a new, or newly up-graded, orchestra primarily for studio broadcasting. It might have seemed a hopeless task. He had long expressed his distaste for recording, though he had (thank heaven) recanted during his last year with the Philharmonic-Symphony. Broadcasting worried him less, perhaps because in those days there seemed no element of permanency about it. His New York concerts had been relayed as a matter of course, and so had his activities in London, Paris and Salzburg. Chotzinoff told how he impressed Toscanini with the importance of bringing great music to the millions as only *he* could do. The NBC Orchestra would be ready for him in Radio City the next winter and he could confine himself to ten weekly broadcasts. There were however to be teething troubles over the formation of the orchestra, which Rodzinski was to audition and prepare, and there were alarm and surprise from the Philharmonic-Symphony. The NBC, it was assured, would not clash or compete with its public concerts (though this was not strictly true) and the live audiences would be confined to non-paying guests. Barbirolli, who was by then in charge of the Philharmonic-Symphony, took the more magnanimous view that whenever Toscanini appeared he raised orchestral standards and that his return to New York would be, at the very least, a mixed blessing.

The preliminary NBC concerts were conducted by Pierre Monteux and Rodzinski. Monteux, a greatly respected conductor in his own right, was one of the many musicians who had been swept off his feet in the nineteen-twenties by Toscanini's gifts, calling him quite simply 'the greatest of all.' Then, on Christmas Day 1937, Toscanini took over and so began an association that was to last for over sixteen years. The programme included Brahms's First and Mozart's G minor symphonies. There have been graphic descriptions of the first rehearsal from players in the NBC, some of whom were interviewed by B H Haggin for his symposium *The Toscanini Musicians Knew*. Two of the violinists, Samuel Antek and Joseph Gingold, spoke of the electrifying effect of the introduction to the Brahms that began the rehearsal, but Gingold's remarks on the Mozart have a special interest: 'I have still to hear a Mozart G minor as great as Toscanini's: in it Mozart emerged in a new light. Toscanini made it a great drama; and I will never forget the opening

phrase – the pathos it had with the inflection he gave.' He added more naively 'It was *his* Mozart; and it was wonderful!' Gingold did admit later that he was upset by Toscanini's behaviour when Bruno Walter came to the NBC as a guest conductor and took a more delicate, some would say more Mozartian, view of the work; but to complete this story Toscanini in his last years recommended Walter's recording of it in preference to his own.

In rehearsal at Carnegie Hall.

Toscanini's reluctance to make commercial records had been waived again through his happy relations with the BBC Orchestra in London, and from 1938 onwards he seemed to accept recording along with broadcasting as a natural way of reaching the masses. Since more and more broadcasts were taken 'live' automatically, some, like the 1939 *Eroica* with the NBC, were approved for issue. During his very first NBC season Toscanini also agreed to actual recording sessions, though the first products, including Haydn's Symphony no 88 and the Mozart G minor, were greeted with some dismay. How it could have happened that such appalling recorded quality could have been allowed by technicians and passed by Toscanini remains a mystery. Most of the blame was attributed to the dry-as-dust acoustics of Studio 8-H and some of it to Toscanini's desire for clarity at all costs; but the horror of the actual sound was only partly alleviated when some sessions were transferred to Carnegie Hall where the natural resonance should have helped. The first *Eroica*, recorded in 8-H with all-too-audible audience noises, proclaimed the worst from the opening chords. It is still an important landmark in the Toscanini discography, and the climax of the double-fugue in the Funeral March is colossal, though the dry sound does nothing to help the mundane quality of some of the wind-playing. A great orchestra cannot be formed overnight, and even with Toscanini's unifying power it took time for the NBC to begin to approach the overall quality of the Philharmonic-Symphony. Some would say that it never did.

Before long Toscanini moved to Carnegie Hall for public performances of the Ninth Symphony and the Verdi *Requiem,* and his second season included concerts in other cities: Boston, Chicago, Pittsburgh. His programmes tended to mix standard classics with light-weight curiosities and were often criticised for their odd juxtapositions. He had his favourite works, like the *Eroica* or *La Mer* or the Brahms 'St Antoni' Variations. Even with his astonishing ear for musical form he accepted such patched-up Wagner extracts as the 'Forest Murmurs' and 'The Ride of the Valkyries'. He played little-known Italians like Martucci or Tommasini but took scant notice of the contemporary cause in general or of leading American composers. There were exceptions, of course. He took to Shostakovitch's First Symphony and during the war gave the first American performances of his Seventh, the 'Leningrad', after a lengthy argument with Stokowski. He did not entirely neglect American music: he liked Samuel Barber's Adagio and played it several times, but Roy Harris's Third Symphony and Copland's *El Salon Mexico* were given only once. Some of his choices were strange indeed: did he need to waste time on Grofé's vulgar and inflated *Grand Canyon Suite?* Gershwin was another matter, and he took *An American in Paris* back to La Scala with him after the war. Spike Hughes wrote that posterity will not want to know *how* Toscanini performed Gershwin or Grofé but *why,* though many musicians would not bracket these two composers.

During his days with the Philharmonic-Symphony Toscanini occasionally included concertos, which could be doubtful blessings for soloists who wished to go their own way. Menuhin, who played the Beethoven concerto with him in 1934, spoke of his meticulous attention to detail including the bowing-marks in the solo part. It was at their preliminary rehearsal with piano that the famous telephone incident occurred: Toscanini, annoyed at the disturbance, eventually ripped the phone from the wall and continued as though nothing had happened. Heifetz recorded the Beethoven with him and the NBC in 1940, and though the sound quality is poor the revelations of balance are remarkable throughout, especially when the orchestra has important themes or counterpoints to play. Two piano concertos, the Brahms B flat and the Tchaikowsky no 1, were recorded about this time with Toscanini's son-in-law Horowitz, though it would be folly to suggest that they were ideally matched partners. Toscanini's unswerving line must have made matters difficult for any soloist, but it was a rare enough experience to hear a large-scale concerto presented as an organic unity with every orchestral detail contributing. Those who relished the fact that the timpani are a bar out halfway through the scherzo of the Brahms, and that Horowitz splits some important notes here and there, might reflect that recording was still a human activity unsullied by such artificial aids to perfection as tape-editing.

There were fewer concertos in the NBC days, partly because programmes

The conductor with Lauritz Melchior and his wife on board the *Bremen*.

were on the whole much shorter, though Toscanini sometimes called on his leading players as soloists, in the Brahms Double, the Mozart Bassoon Concerto and so forth. Among pianists he admired Ania Dorfman and Mieczylaw Horzowski, who pleased him by learning the Martucci concerto. Horzowski told me a story about the Mozart B flat Concerto K595 that testifies to Toscanini's extraordinary memory. It is now generally agreed that seven bars are missing from the middle of the first tutti as printed in the older editions, but how to broach this subject at rehearsal? Toscanini however went rapidly through the score in his head and immediately detected the place through awkwardness in the part-writing. Since tempo was of vital importance to Toscanini and he was uncompromising by nature there could be serious problems with a concerto soloist who held different views. In 1946 he invited Dame Myra Hess to play the Beethoven 'Emperor' with him, partly maybe because of his admiration for her wartime organisation of the National Gallery Concerts in London. She told me of her trepidation. Knowing his reputation for fast tempi she practised the passage with left-hand triplets in the first movement up to her top form and, to his approval, threw it off at breakneck speed when they met for a discussion. She then persuaded him to change to the Beethoven C minor! At the final rehearsal he brought in the orchestra four bars too soon in the slow movement, and a glance at the full score will show how easy it is to confuse two similar cadences. The likeness of the missing solo phrases to 'Salve! Dimora casta e pura' from Gounod's *Faust*

With his wife, Signora Carla Toscanini, in 1940.

had often struck her and she asked Toscanini to 'let her sing' her cavatina at the performance. At first he was amused at his lapse and her request, but he was soon furious with himself: 'I say terrible things about other conductors, but I cannot conduct myself!'

In 1940 Toscanini had taken the NBC Orchestra on a tour of South America, giving sixteen concerts in Rio, Sao Paulo, Buenos Aires and Montevideo – memories of old haunts! – and in 1950 he was to tour the States with them. (It is curious how the ten-year pattern of touring repeated itself: in 1920 he took the Scala Orchestra to America, and in 1930 the New York Philharmonic-Symphony to Europe.) During the war he had however run into trouble with the NBC organisers over the engagement of personnel and over the players' other commitments. In 1941 there were rumours of his resignation. The temporary break enabled him to take on more guest appearances elsewhere, such as a Beethoven cycle with the Philharmonic-Symphony and a series of concerts with the Philadelphia Orchestra. His recordings with the Philadelphia were ill-fated: some sides he did not approve, others were mechanically defective, and a Union ban intervened to prevent him re-recording them. Their long-delayed issue showed how this magnificent orchestra, brought up on Stokowski and Ormandy, responded to produce the purity and clarity of the Toscanini 'sound'. Sol Schoenbach, the first bassoon, had reservations about Toscanini's playing of Romantic music, which had been Stokowski's speciality, but he told B H Haggin: [24]

> With Toscanini it's the drive and intensity I keep coming back to. Though he didn't have the greatest technique with the stick, it certainly was adequate for everything that had to be done. But I think it was his personality more than his technique that enabled him to hold huge forces together in concentration.

What however is technique if not simply a means to an end? Bernard Shore wrote about this in *The Orchestra Speaks:* [25]

> First is the magnificent sweep, which must be one of the most eloquent gestures ever made and which seems to hold all the threads of the orchestra and to imbue them with life. Secondly, there is his not so apparent, but extraordinarily dynamic, almost magical preparation for his beats.

To the onlooker Toscanini's gestures seemed a natural expression of his wishes. His stick did not in fact 'beat time' but was like an extension of his personality, engaging in no mechanical tricks, clicks or self-conscious subdivisions. Lauri Kennedy, who led the cellos in Toscanini's first two seasons with the BBC in London, spoke about the confidence he instilled in most of the players, the feeling that they would have *time* to play every note. Yet he did not appear to eliminate risks. The circular motions that his baton described instinctively in strongly continuing rhythms, as in Beethoven's scherzos, gave the music an irresistible forward movement, but his ear appeared to control every strand of the texture independently. Dennis Brain said that when Toscanini rehearsed the Brahms symphonies with the Philharmonia Orchestra in 1952 and approached a passage where the horns usually anticipate a crescendo his hand seemed to reach across the orchestra to him as though to warn 'take care!'. The gesture was in fact no more than a flicker but the message was conveyed.

Toscanini returned to the NBC for occasional war charity concerts during the 1941-42 season and took over a full schedule again the following year. He had a renewed desire to conduct opera again and, with news of the downfall of Mussolini, his intense patriotism flared into life in programmes of Verdi extracts. It was then that he adapted Verdi's *Hymn of the Nations* for a propaganda film sponsored by the US Office of War Information. He also included it in a remarkable concert at Madison Square Garden on 25 May 1944 in aid of the Red Cross. The programme was Wagner *and* Verdi, and it was enhanced by the combined NBC and Philharmonic-Symphony orchestras. The last act of *Rigoletto*, with Milanov, Merriman, Peerce, Warren and Moscona, was later issued in a recorded Toscanini Anthology. To achieve such compelling drama, let alone the fire and precision, in a concert performance was astounding and gives some idea perhaps of the impact Toscanini made with the earlier Verdi at La Scala and the Met. It is significant that his Beethoven series later that year included a complete *Fidelio*. This was the first of seven operas that he conducted in concert form between 1944 and 1954, each broadcast in two weekly instalments.

Meanwhile the end of the war in Europe was celebrated with a broadcast of Beethoven's Fifth, and on that same day, 18 May 1945, Toscanini began a long series of recording sessions that took him through the summer. His recorded repertory, to be supplemented vastly by official and unofficial recordings from broadcasts, became more catholic and more curious. It ranged that year from Haydn's Symphony no 98, Mozart's 'Jupiter' and Beethoven's Seventh (which was not issued) to Rossini overtures, which were always welcome from him, Waldteufel's *Skaters' Waltz* and Sousa's *Stars and Stripes*. This last was always an exhilarating experience from him, especially in the clarity yet abandon of its final combination of themes. His way with popular miniatures was like that of a great virtuoso playing on a single instrument, and during the war he gave whole programmes of such pieces. Boccherini's celebrated Minuet and Ponchielli's *Dance of the Hours* could not have been performed with more spontaneous charm. It was more dubious when he played isolated movements from the Beethoven quartets, or his complete Septet, with orchestral forces, though the desire to involve himself in works he had loved from his youth was strong. Taubman reported that he wanted, with more justification, to perform a movement from a long-forgotten quartet by Raff and wrote out the score from memory, complete with expression marks. When a copy was unearthed he was found to have

86

A studio performance of *Aida* (March-April 1949) with Nelli, Tucker, Scott, Valdengo and Gustavson as soloists.

made *one* mistake – but he never actually played the piece.

As 1946 was the fiftieth anniversary of his première of *La Bohème*, Toscanini appropriately chose it as his second complete opera with the NBC. There is no point in comparing the recording with better-sounding ones or more favourite singers. In the best sense of the term 'tradition' it is fascinating, and from the musical and dramatic sides incomparable in its alternations of vigour and pathos. Mimi's entrance in the last act could never have seemed more of a reality in the opera-house. Jan Peerce, who sang Rodolfo, remarked on Toscanini's own singing which was more audible than usual and irritated some critics. 'For me it makes the record' Peerce said. At the end Toscanini was overcome with emotion and the brass mistook his cue. It ruined the whole performance for him and he refused to take a bow, though for posterity he was able to re-make the closing bars just as he was to do, five years after the event, with parts of *Aida*.

That summer he returned in triumph to La Scala and thereafter divided his time between New York and Italy where he spent his vacations and gave occasional concerts. His remaining opera broadcasts for the NBC were all Verdi: *Traviata, Otello, Aida, Falstaff, Ballo*. He led a further eight seasons and in 1950 amazed everyone with the energy he still summoned on his six-week coast-to-coast tour of the States. John Rosenfield, a Texan music critic, wrote: [26]

Three generations at New Orleans: Walter, Arturo and Walfredo Toscanini during a national tour given by The NBC Symphony Orchestra (April 1950).

> No other conductor of musical history has obtained comparable immortality during or after his lifetime. . . . He carries his greatness not in lonely splendour, but as a vividly human being among fellow creatures.

His programmes were conservative but varied, and he added 'Dixie' to his repertory with resounding success.

Toscanini's powers in old age continued to thrive and amaze. Some critics, including his most fervent admirers, felt at times that a sense of desperation crept into some of his later performances. His passion for realising a work as an indivisible unity could lead him to press forwards in order to encompass it, as it were, in a single thought. Hence there were complaints, sometimes justified, that he played some works faster, in fact too fast, as time went on. In his *Traviata* recording of 1946 he was accused of tyrannising the singers to the extent of disregarding Verdi's own markings. Spike Hughes, who was never reticent about what he considered Toscanini's shortcomings, sprang to defend this *Traviata* on the grounds that it was conducted not as a singers' opera, nor even as a conductor's opera, but as a composer's opera, and he called in the score as evidence. The real danger in assessing those later NBC years is to generalise. Not all Toscanini's tempi became faster: some works, like the Brahms Tragic Overture, were broadened in conception. There was

Bronze bust of Toscanini by Troubetskoy.

however a general tendency to tighten the reins and refine away certain freedoms that, strict as he may have seemed to others, he had allowed himself in the nineteen-thirties, for example. There is irony in the fact that a great conductor who had fought shy of the microphone for so many years should have spent most of his last sixteen years in front of one. Even when his broadcasts were transferred to Carnegie Hall the possibility of eternal play-backs and post-mortems could have a subtly insidious effect. On the whole subject of recording Alfred Wallenstein, who had been first cellist under him in the Philharmonic-Symphony days, wrote:[27]

But some of his greatest performances didn't get recorded; and some of the performances that did get recorded give a wrong impression to someone who doesn't know all his work. I don't think he was well served by his recordings – on the basis of sound and other things. . . . For him recording was the most difficult thing in the world; because it made him tense. Any audience didn't disturb him; but the microphone did; and so the performance he recorded was sometimes a little fast, sometimes a little slow.

This is not to belittle the colossal value of most of those later NBC recordings but simply to answer (and even to agree with) frequent criticisms of them.

In 1949 Toscanini slipped in his bath and bruised a rib, and in 1950 suffered from recurring knee pains. The following year, while exercising his knee, he had a minor stroke, which meant cancelling his plans for that summer, including the opening of the Royal Festival Hall in London. His resilience was such that he was able to take on a busier season than ever the following winter with numerous recording sessions of large-scale works ending with Beethoven's Ninth. A year later, almost to the day, he recorded the *Missa Solemnis* after a hardly less exacting season. Harvey Sachs made some interesting comparisons between the officially available 1953 *Missa* and 'pirate' copies taken from the air of Toscanini performances in 1935 and 1940. He ended by preferring the earliest, not only over the question of tempo but of character and conception. There was, as may be noted in other works, a breadth and grandeur in 1935 that became tightened up by a gradual process of 'simplification'. The quest for a kind of definitive perfection in which rhetorical gestures were refined away must have haunted Toscanini in those later years. The records of the Ninth and the *Missa* are still invaluable documents, though for many people the 'classic' Beethoven performance of Toscanini remains the 1936 Seventh Symphony. Ironically and sadly he spent hours after his retirement listening to his records and wishing to destroy most of them, though the season leading up to his tragic final concert showed him for much of the time at the very height of his powers.

There was for example a remarkable performance of Strauss's *Don Quixote* with Frank Miller and Carlton Cooley in the first broadcast of that season, but it is to Verdi that one turns for Toscanini's most moving valedictions. On 17 and 24 January 1954 he conducted his last complete opera. He chose *Un Ballo in Maschera*, which as he recalled was the first opera he had ever heard at the Regio in Parma eighty-three years before. After the second broadcast, which as usual took place before an audience in Carnegie Hall, the London *Times* correspondent wrote:[28]

There could be no more moving sight than that of Toscanini's tiny, frail figure producing, with an economy of gesture eloquent of infinite pains in rehearsal, performances that will probably never be equalled in brilliance and dramatic power. The orchestra plays for him as it plays for nobody else, and singers obey him, as the *New York Times* says this morning "not only as if they would lose their lives if they did not, but as if they would gladly give their lives for him if they had to do so."

Almost as a kind of postscript to this Verdi tribute he gave an equally unforgettable performance of the *Te Deum* in March, along with the Prologue to Boito's *Mefistofele*. The spiritual quality and the human warmth were unbearably moving and Toscanini's control of the large forces was supreme. Three weeks later he ended the season, and his public career, with an all-Wagner programme.

He knew that this was to be his last concert with the NBC and that this meant the disbanding of the orchestra, though his retirement had not been announced. The rehearsals were stormy; and at the concert he stopped conducting after the great climax in the Venusberg Music from *Tannhäuser*. The music literally disintegrated for a while until he recovered himself sufficiently to pick up the threads and finish, or almost finish the programme. He dropped his baton and left the platform as the orchestra played the final chords of the *Meistersinger* Prelude. His conducting début had been dramatic and his farewell was tragically so. He returned to the orchestra that summer to re-make parts of *Aida* and *Ballo* and surprised the players with his rejuvenation. He never conducted again, though he wanted to do so. The NBC Orchestra re-formed itself as 'The Symphony of the Air' and begged him to return, but in vain. It gave its first concert the following October without a conductor. The members informed Toscanini that 'we have decided to play our concert with the podium empty with only the inspirational memory of your guiding hands before us. . . .'

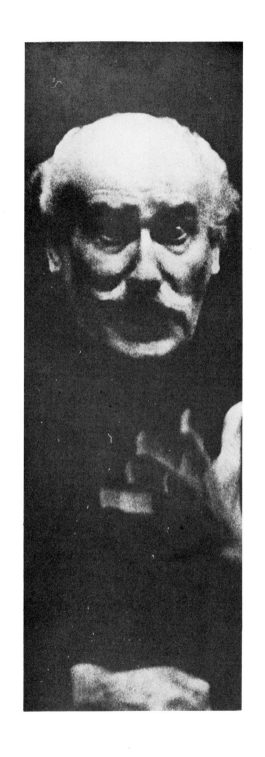

Chapter Seven

'RITORNI TOSCANINI'

When Mussolini's downfall was announced on 25 July 1943 Toscanini was conducting a programme of Verdi extracts in New York. In Milan, as though by magic, placards printed with the slogans 'Evviva Toscanini' and 'Ritorni Toscanini' appeared on the walls of La Scala. It was fourteen years since he had resigned its directorship and twelve since his confrontation with the Fascists in Bologna. During the war his name had become a symbol of liberty and anti-Fascism. Italian music-lovers, divorced from his art for so long, clamoured for his return. In America he had published his views on a 'free' Italy, which included the abolition of the monarchy that had tacitly supported the Mussolini régime. Meanwhile La Scala fell a victim to Allied bombs within a month of the appearance of the Toscanini placards but its reconstruction began immediately the war was over. In April 1946 Toscanini returned to Milan to prepare for the re-opening. On 11 May he conducted a massive programme devoted to the masters of Italian opera he had served so well: Rossini, Verdi, Puccini, Boito. The overture to *La Gazza Ladra* at once proclaimed that age had not lessened his rhythmic fire. The rehearsals, as of old, had their moments of storm. Enrico Minetti, who led the orchestra and had played in it when Toscanini re-formed it after the First World War, smiled at the consternation of the younger members: 'At last we had found "our" Maestro again, just as we remembered him from distant times, just as we had known, admired, feared and loved him.' The programme brought back so many memories of his past associations with La Scala: the Verdi *Te Deum* and the Prologue to Boito's *Mefistofele;* two moving extracts from operas he had never actually produced, the Prayer from Rossini's *Mose* and the Slaves' Chorus from Verdi's early *Nabucco;* and the third act of *Manon Lescaut,* for which he had received such praise from Puccini in the nineteen-twenties.

Seven concerts were planned for the re-opening festivities, two of them conducted by Mitropoulos and one by Antonino Votto, who had been Toscanini's friend and assistant quarter-of-a-century before. The second programme included Brahms's Third Symphony and Debussy's *La Mer.* It took only a bar or two of the Brahms, picked up on an Italian wave-length, to reveal that Toscanini was in charge. (The exact bars were 33 to 40 in the slow movement, a transitional passage that sometimes goes for nothing, but on this occasion and heard from afar, as it were, the balance and timing were

Toscanini's summer retreat on the Isolino San Giovanni.

arrestingly beautiful.) Toscanini also conducted Beethoven's First and Ninth symphonies in the final concert which, like part of the opening one, was relayed to British listeners. There then came the bitter disappointment of the proposed Paris and London concerts which Toscanini cancelled owing to the 'new humiliations' Italy was alleged to feel over the ceding of Briga and Tenda to France. The concerts he gave in Lucerne instead have been mentioned elsewhere. At the time Walter Legge was in Zürich supervising recordings for EMI, including some by a newly-discovered young Rumanian pianist called Dinu Lipatti. I also accompanied some Schumann songs for the soprano Maria Reining, who had sung Eva in Toscanini's 1937 *Meistersinger* at Salzburg. Realising that Toscanini was in fact 'on the air' at that very moment, Legge had recordings taken from the Lucerne broadcasts and played them to me on our return to London. The second concert, which I attended, contained wonderful performances of the overture *Leonore no 2* and the Paris version of the *Tannhäuser* Venusberg Music. The Wagner was a Toscanini revelation that he never recorded officially, unless one includes his last-of-all tragic performance with the NBC.

It was hoped, of course, that Toscanini's post-war visits to Europe would yield more than they did, but apart from his Philharmonia concerts in 1952 and the Lucerne ones of 1946 they were confined to occasional events at La Scala and one at La Fenice in Venice. In 1948 he devoted a whole programme

On the terrace, overlooking Lake Maggiore.

to Boito, who had supported him so strongly on his first appointment to La Scala half-a-century before. And in 1949? Some excuse may be required for continuing on a more personal note, though the following adventure might be regarded as symbolic of the quite unusual reverence that countless music-lovers have felt for the art of Toscanini.

In August 1949 I was on holiday in Italy and chanced on a fairly routine performance of *Rigoletto* in Florence. It was *not* conducted by him, I hasten to add; but listening to Verdi for the first time in their native land prompted the solitary thought – Toscanini. Rumours had spread that he was spending his customary vacation in Milan after his usual NBC season in New York, and as these respites often included a concert or concerts with the Scala Orchestra I decided to investigate. The desire to meet him was strong. I wanted to thank him in person for his unique service to music, to try and persuade him to conduct in England again, and even entertained the faint hope of fathoming some of his extraordinary personality. I knew however that he was not easily accessible to strangers, since he hated interviews and publicity and was jealously guarded by his family and close friends. I had read somewhere that after the war he had gone back to his old home in the Via Durini, and on arrival in Milan booked in at a nearby hotel, the Francia; but it was with a trembling hand that I dared to knock on the door of the famous residence. There appeared a middle-aged woman dressed in black, apparently the lodge-keeper or suchlike, and she let forth a stream of voluble Italian that I could only stem by asking 'the Maestro?' She then examined me more closely, put her hands to her sides and laughed raucously as though to say 'and who do you think you are?' But one word she repeated, enabling me to catch it as evidence that Toscanini was not there; and she made a scribbling sign which on my producing pencil and paper revealed the word 'Pallanza'. I returned to the hotel and showed it to the hall porter, who spoke English and explained: 'Ah, yes – Pallanza, on the Lago Maggiore! I will show you on the map. Go to the lake beyond Stresa and take lunch at the Grand Albergo Maestoso. Ask the manager to direct you to the Toscanini villa.'

I had not bargained for the villa being on its own island, the Isolino San Giovanni, admittedly within swimming distance but obviously sacrosanct. The manager asked my purpose and I explained that I was simply an English musician who wanted to meet the Maestro for a moment in order to give him greetings in person from some of his London friends. This was only an excuse, but both Dame Myra Hess and Sir Adrian Boult had told me that I might use their names in such a case. 'Well, if you really *are* a musician. . . .' the manager continued, and I was told how that very morning the Old Man, who came to the lake for peace and was shy of strangers at the best of times, had woken in a good mood and agreed to see some so-called music-lovers who had been waiting at the hotel in hopes. 'And what happens? They produce flash-light cameras and bombard him with stupid questions like a press interview. So he retires to his study and locks the door – can you blame him?' I felt my own hopes dwindling but the manager went on: 'Perhaps the time is not right, but I tell you that at three o'clock this afternoon the Maestro's wife Donna Carla and her sister are coming on a boat-trip down the lake with some of the hotel guests. If you like to come too, I will try to arrange that you sit next to her when we stop to take tea on the Isola Madre. The rest is up to you!'

After an interminable expedition, with myself hiding inconspicuously in the crowd, tea was at last served and I noted with relief a glimmer of hope in the eyes of the hotel manager, who had accompanied the party. He beckoned and then introduced me to Donna Carla, presumably having forewarned her. She apparently spoke no English, which surprised me since she must have spent nearly half her life in New York, and as my Italian was largely confined to titles of operatic arias and musical terms we began to converse in tentative French. Almost at once there came a propitious question, as if to sound me out: did I like *Falstaff?* I was able to answer in truth that it had been my favourite Verdi opera ever since I heard Toscanini conduct it at Salzburg in 1937 with Stabile in the title-role. This was a good start, and before long we were having our photograph taken together! Our conversation continued back on the boat and I told her frankly that I had always loved the Maestro's work so much that I would give years of my life to be able to meet him. By this time we were back at the landing-stage of the hotel, and as Donna Carla stepped

The main bedroom at Isolino San Giovanni.

into the little rowing-boat to return to the Isolino she said 'If it is possible we will telephone within quarter of an hour. There is no point in waiting longer.'

The manager hinted that this was not a novel situation, and he was not optimistic as he went upstairs to his office; but almost immediately he was running down again shouting 'You are a lucky man – they are sending the boat again!' And there, sure enough, was the little ragazzo chasing down the hillside of the island and launching his oars for the second time. The setting could not have been more romantic, with the clear Italian sky beginning to deepen its blue against the mountains. Five minutes later I was bounding up the wooded path in pursuit of my guide, when quite suddenly there was the terrace and Donna Carla coming to meet me, and Toscanini himself, absorbed in the view, his face of indescribable beauty and sadness. Yet when he turned to greet me it adopted a shy, awkward expression as of a child warned to be on his best behaviour when talking to a forbidding aunt. We went inside at once and the Maestro, in a gentle but husky voice, began to ask me about my visit. Had I been to Italy before? What art galleries had I seen?

97

Then he talked about England, and I gave him Dame Myra's greetings. 'She is playing a lot?' he asked. I nodded. 'And the BBC Orchestra – is Boult still with them?' 'They are all waiting for you to come back!' 'I remember the good chorus-master they had for the Verdi *Requiem*' he said. 'Leslie Woodgate' I replied. We then discussed the problem of concert-halls in London, since the Queen's Hall had been destroyed during the war, and he was now able to joke about the acoustics of the old Albert Hall over which he had despaired on his tour with the New York Philharmonic-Symphony.

He then asked 'and what about this new orchestra of Beecham's: the Royal Philharmonic?' He went on with a rather mischievous smile creeping in for the first time: 'I always think there is something a little mad about Beecham?' This I felt was a tricky subject to pursue, so I forbore to mention Mozart and said simply that genius was sometimes unaccountable, and he smiled again. He then relapsed into sadness again and murmured almost under his breath that he was so ashamed to be old and to have so much more to learn. I assured him of the devotion still felt by his English listeners even though he had not been to London for ten years; and marvelled that this frail figure with its

With Yehudi Menuhin, one of many distinguished visitors at the Isolino San Giovanni.

98

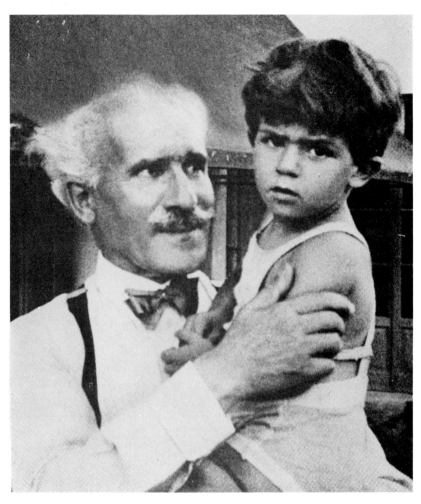

Toscanini with his grandson, Walfredo.

nervously shifting eyes, that yet seemed so magnetic in their momentary rests, could summon such compelling unanimity from orchestra when our tête-à-tête was interrupted by the arrival of an expected visitor, Antonio Ghiringhelli, director of La Scala. This gave me my cue to retire while he talked business with the Maestro, or so I assumed from the heat that was suddenly engendered. 'They are discussing some forthcoming concerts in aid of the Scala rebuilding fund' said Toscanini's elder daughter Wally, who now befriended me. 'The first concert is in Venice, the second in Milan. Can't you come? I will arrange for tickets to be left in your name.' Meanwhile I was startled at the change in the Maestro, who was waxing vehement about certain changes in the Scala Orchestra. Even discussion of musical matters was enough, apparently, to turn a frail old man into a living flame. 'My father looks well, don't you think?' said Wally, though never having been so close to a human volcano before made comparisons difficult.

As soon as Ghiringhelli had departed we all went out on the terrace again, and as I took my leave Toscanini said once more 'I am old and you are young – how lucky you are!' 'Please come to London soon!' I begged, as my young oarsman reappeared to take me back to the hotel. This informal encounter meant a great deal to one who had so often admired Toscanini's work from afar. He was not only a phenomenon and a legend, a touchstone of musical honesty and a fantastic example of tireless endeavour. He was above all a human being, with human limitations and maybe human failings. Even in old age he confessed that he had so much to learn, and he knew that time was short. That is why I spared no effort and expense to return to Italy for his concerts in Venice and Milan, even though they were not, as it turned out, the most memorable I experienced from him.

The Teatro La Fenice was garlanded with roses for the occasion, though the audience was one of those notoriously noisy Italian ones quite out of keeping with the type of music-making that was taking place. Sitting on the stage behind the orchestra may not be ideal for sound, but gave a splendid opportunity of seeing those sparing but eloquent gestures that were always the antithesis of the methods of most other precision-bound conductors. Although it was uncomfortably hot, I noted at the time that everyone was silenced by the breath-taking string crescendos in Cherubini's *Anacreon* overture; and the obvious popular appeal of *Vltava* called forth shouts of 'grazie, grazie' from all directions. *Don Juan,* too, was stunning in its abandon, overwhelming at the climaxes, yet never ceasing for one moment to 'sing' and as clear, even from back-stage, as the finest playing of a Bach five-part fugue. Beethoven's *Pastoral* Symphony, on the other hand, seemed to suffer both from the heat and Toscanini's forward-looking impulse, and his own unhappiness was not alleviated by the flashing of cameras that greeted its close.

The Milan concert five days later – on 8 September 1949 – was like a superior replica of the Venice one, except that the Cherubini was replaced with Beethoven's *Zur Weihe des Hauses,* an excellent occasional piece in which the 'con brio' of the fugato was taken literally, and why not? When one hears the traditionally pompous four-square reading of this volatile late-Beethoven transformation of a Handelian style one is tempted to say 'go to Italy', as Beethoven is supposed to have said on the subject of performances of his quartets. At the recapitulation the violins threw up an arch of counterpoint that in its long phrasing reminded me of Schnabel's precipitate tempo in the first movement of the 'Hammerklavier' Sonata. Both programmes included Franck's *Les Eolides.* How is it that a supreme interpreter can command interest, even move one to tears, in music that normally leaves one rather indifferent?

100

It was after his return to America that he received a cable from the Italian President Einaudi offering him a life appointment to the Senate. Although he had often been accused of meddling in politics, as over the French-Italian border affair, he was shy of any kind of political or academic honour and declined: [29]

> I would like to end my life in the same simple way in which I have lived it. I am grateful and happy for the recognition shown by my country and am ready to serve it again in any event. I beg you not to interpret my refusal as discourteous or proud, but rather in the spirit of simplicity and modesty that inspires it.

He continued to spend his summers in Italy. In 1950 he conducted the Verdi *Requiem* at La Scala but was more than usually displeased; in 1951 he was unwell and had to cancel his plans to visit London and to conduct *Falstaff* at Busseto, but made records of the *Traviata* Preludes with the Scala Orchestra in aid of the Casa Verdi – which were only issued in Brazil! His last Milan concert was in 1952 and, as fate arranged it, an all-Wagner one, given only a few days before his Brahms concerts in London. After his dramatic retirement from the NBC in 1954 he went back again to Italy and still had thoughts of conducting opera again in a small theatre, perhaps Puccini's *La Rondine* but above all *Falstaff*. La Scala was building such a theatre, the Piccola Scala, and there were rumours that he would conduct at its opening, but the excitement and anxiety gave him a heart attack. He returned to New York in February 1955, faced the fact that he would never conduct again and with his son Walter spent hours over the editing of his records, suffering moods when he wished to destroy them all. Young and old friends visited him and played to him, and in turn he talked music with them and drew on his still astounding memory. One young conductor he admired and helped, Guido Cantelli, was killed in a plane crash in November 1956 but the news was kept from Toscanini. He died himself less than two months later on 16 January 1957. His body was flown to Milan and buried in the family tomb to the sound of 'Va, pensiero' from *Nabucco* which he had conducted there in 1901 after the death of Verdi.

Chapter Eight

TOSCANINI AND THE CRITICS

Toscanini seldom gave interviews, but after one of his BBC concerts in London he agreed to go with Sir Adrian Boult to a press conference. C B Rees reported in *Radio Times* on an amusing reply to a question about which work the orchestra had played best. 'You are a critic?' asked Toscanini. 'Then – *you* know!' he added. How seriously he took press criticism in general it is hard to ascertain, though in spite of his supposed half-blindness he read a great deal apart from musical scores. In 1911 Busoni was amazed to hear him quoting whole pages from memory of his own recent book on musical aesthetics. Toscanini's friends Georgina and Owen Mase told me of his love for English poetry, which he would recite at length and *in* English. Of writers on music he thought little of Schumann the critic, but delighted in Mozart's letters, studied the writings of Wagner and Verdi, admired Tovey's essays, and showed the power of instant recall that had been noted since his early schooldays. What of his own critics? The pattern of Toscanini criticism over the years has always been one of stunned admiration offset by a few equally extravagant denials. He must have been fully aware of the factions that rebelled against his uncompromising nature and the undiluted adulation he inspired. In 1930, the year of his legendary tour with the New York Philharmonic-Symphony, the American critic Edward Robinson wrote that Toscanini had 'the single, phenomenal capacity for maintaining a persistent tempo with the mechanical rigidity of a metronome.' Listeners to his early recording of the 'Haffner' Symphony please note!

There was prejudice involved here. Robinson admired Mengelberg, who had been edged out of the New York scene by Toscanini's successes. The story is told of their opposite approaches to the *Coriolan* overture, Mengelberg insisting that he had inherited the true German tradition through a personal handing-down from Beethoven, and Toscanini saying that he had it direct from Beethoven himself – from the score. The old argument of 'objective' versus 'subjective' may seem too facile, but there is a strong element of truth in it, as Klemperer indicated when he called Toscanini 'the ideal representative of objectivity.' In this respect Furtwängler is usually held up as the antithesis of Toscanini, and friendships may have been broken over their merits and demerits. Why not Toscanini *and* Furtwängler, one might well ask? Yet it seems that differing ideals and blazing visions, in art as in politics, are liable to be mutually exclusive. To the partisans Furtwängler was

In rehearsal with The NBC Symphony Orchestra.

either a profound interpreter or the epitome of self-indulgence, and Toscanini a saviour or a time-beater.

The myth of the human metronome dates back at least as far as Giulio Ricordi, who tried to prevent Toscanini's revival of *Trovatore* at La Scala in 1902. Is it likely that the public and the other critics would have reacted so ecstatically to a metronomisation of their beloved Verdi? Adherence to a basic tempo was however one of Toscanini's first principles and closely related to his 'objectivity', aided by his near-perfect sense of rhythm and timing. Playing in time or 'as written' was, as has been said, illusory, taking no account of the infinite subtleties of balance, accentuation and long phrasing that were hallmarks of Toscanini's performances. It is true that in some works he allowed far greater flexibility in his sixties than his eighties, as recordings show, and it was also true that where the music called for a continuous rhythmic impetus he was able to carry it through with a superhuman energy and control. In slower music too the relation of line to a basic pulse had a phenomenal effect, as happened with the Prelude to *Lohengrin*, which led towards and away from its climax with a constantly glowing sonority, unfolding itself in unbroken unity. Egon Petri spoke of the feeling of inevitability about such performances, a quality that might be emulated or striven after, but scarcely imitated. The young conductors who practised beating time to Toscanini's records were simply clipping their own wings, and he was sometimes blamed for his deceptively dangerous influence. The conductor Josef Krips said that the one thing from which all could learn was 'devotion to the composer', but to some ears this had a touch of sanctimony about it, like Toscanini's own remark 'just an honest musician'. The implication that no-one else was devoted or honest was easily read into this as part of the Toscanini cult.

104

Adverse criticism has tended to focus on two things in particular as qualities carried to excess. One was the intense fervour of Toscanini's approach in general, the other his supposed predilection for fast tempi. When his earlier recording of Brahms's First Symphony appeared, a conductor friend of mine, having chastised Toscanini for adding drumrolls to the chorale at the end, complained: 'Where I wanted rhythm I found it, where I wanted clarity I found it, where I wanted expression I found it – but it was all too intense, inhuman in fact.' It was an absolutely valid criticism to find that Toscanini's intensity ruled out qualities of mystery and resignation that others read into the work. This had been many people's objection to his Mozart, especially the G minor Symphony, but even his Verdi came under occasional attack, and not only from Giulio Ricordi, for his tyranny over the singers. Of course where tradition had yielded to vanity or self-indulgence Toscanini would inevitably seem brusque, though this impression quickly evaporated on a second or third hearing. This raises the more general question of tempo and the illusion of speed that could arise through vitality and clarity and harmonic progression.

It was in fact part truth, part illusion. His *Parsifal* at Bayreuth was by far the slowest known there, and in the nineteen-thirties he took five-and-a-half minutes longer than Koussevitsky over the Funeral March of the *Eroica*, though no-one complained of its slowness. During his visits to the BBC, however, he did ask Sir Arthur Bliss: 'Do *you*, as an English musician, think that I, as an Italian, take the slow movements of Beethoven rather fast?' Bliss was impressed with Toscanini's modesty but did not quote his reply. The Fourth Symphony, perhaps, which seemed more andante than adagio? The Seventh was another matter, where his quicker tempi in the second movement and the trio of the scherzo should have debunked lethargic traditions for good. Traditions however may hang heavily and even justified departures may receive dissent and dismay. The slow movement of the great C major Schubert was another case where tradition received an initial shock, though it took only a few bars to absorb one in the flow and texture of the music. It is not that Toscanini's tempo as such was 'right' – many would say it was too fast despite the marking 'andante con moto' – but that the integration of detail and propulsion of the whole produced the feeling of 'rightness'.

The impression or illusion of rightness (Klemperer's word) was brought about because of Toscanini's unique power of striking home on many counts simultaneously: the spirit and the letter, the manifestation of beauty and the unanimity of the response. So often he seemed the personification of Tovey's well-known maxim: 'Never believe that accuracy is dull; on the contrary, dullness is usually full of mean little inaccuracies.' Near the beginning of the Verdi *Requiem* the music moves from A minor to A major just before the words 'et lux'. How tempting to underline the crescendo and rinforzando in the strings with a ritardando and to make an artificial break before the sudden quietness of the major key! Yet Toscanini sought the truth, removed all trace

of sentimentality, and produced an effect of tenderness and awe that transmitted itself to the players. Then turn to the 'Libera me' at the end of the *Requiem* and the results of precise observation and accuracy in a very different context. How one heard, in the hall with no trick of balance, every one of the woodwind counterpoints at the resumption of the fugato was a physiological phenomenon but by no means unique in one's experience of Toscanini; the great *tutta forza* climax was strengthened by being taken in strict tempo; and the slight broadening of the final cadence after the soprano's high C was thereby double effective. Or take the coda of the Ninth Symphony, where Toscanini held the rhythm firmly and allowed the diminutions and the closing triplet figure to make their points with Classical precision, in marked contrast to Furtwängler's hectic and vulgar 'grandstand' finish. The opening of the Ninth however summed up the pros and cons of these different approaches. Should one actually *hear* that there are six notes to a beat in the string tremolos – or did Beethoven want a clouded effect, in which case Toscanini was *too* clear?

Yet clarity of texture was one of the most remarkable of his qualities, enabling one to follow every thread of the composer's thought. It was this no doubt that Ernest Bloch referred to when he said that Toscanini had given him *all the music* of the *Tristan* Prelude. Others, like James Agate, might find a defect in its very virtue: 'I heard things in the score' he wrote 'and didn't want to hear them!' Some critics found such clarity specifically Italian. Frank Howes of *The Times* described Toscanini's *Meistersinger* overture as 'a pageant of Florentine nobles'. Neville Cardus rightly refused to have his critical faculty blunted by the myth of infallibility, admiring Toscanini's noble reading of the Ninth Symphony but not 'his ungenial and rigid hammering-out' of the Seventh. Bernard Keeffe, in a centenary broadcast assessment, spoke of Toscanini's mastery of the *materials* of music, with reservations about style and tone-colour, and about his latter-day tendency to 'steam-roller' works he had played too often. It is possible to see a grain of truth in these strictures without agreeing with them: to find the Seventh Symphony not ungenial but elemental, and to admire the extraordinary *range* of style and colour in works from Vivaldi to Debussy. If Toscanini seldom talked about 'tone-colour' at rehearsal it was because his gestures alone sufficed. Robert Shaw referred to his effect on the choir in the Prologue to *Mefistofele:*[30]

> In immediate response to his gesture the tone of the choir got richer and deeper and broader – a staggering thing which never happened with another conductor. In general, vocal sound, when it's in blocks of sixty people, remains what it is: you can't get a college glee club to change this tone just by gesture; you can do it by exercises or by telling them what you want. But with Toscanini the tone changed in immediate response to his gesture.

As for the suggestion that Toscanini 'Italianised' the German classics, Ernest Newman wrote to me:[31]

> I thought I had lived so long and learned so much about human imbecility that nothing could surprise me: but to discover that there are people going about believing that Toscanini conducts Beethoven like Rossini, and who are still uncertified, bowls me over. The only conclusion I can come to is that their relatives have influence with the Lunacy Commissioners.

There is however the argument that a great deal of music benefits from complementary qualities in its interpretation, such as a strong sense of form in Romantic works and a Romantic warmth in the earlier Classics, but from this point of view Toscanini's own gifts were themselves complementary. T W Gervais in the fifth edition of Grove's Dictionary summed this up well in a single sentence: 'Perhaps his outstanding virtue is an almost unique fusion of the intensest emotional fire with the most luminous intellectual logic and subtlety.' Moreover the logic and subtlety extended to a work as a whole: [32]

> It has been said too often that he 'adds nothing to the score'; this is ambiguous, and is a tribute rather to his powerful sense of musical structure, which preserves a single curve even for an entire opera, so that every note seems a cell in one stupendous, almost geometrical organism.

It was this overriding quality of unity of form and spirit that was served by his other manifold gifts. On the one hand *The Musical Times* reported on the often-heard comment that 'the orchestra had played brilliantly' or 'a piece of music had never sounded so thrilling'. Bonavia of the London *Daily Telegraph* hinted cautiously at something more definitive: [33]

> A great work of art, like a great philosophical system, admits of varied interpretations, and just as there is no reason to suppose that Jowett has said the last word on Plato, so we have no right to think that any interpretation of a Beethoven symphony is 'final', even though Toscanini does sometimes suggest finality.

Bonavia reiterated the much-used words about 'honesty, integrity and unswerving devotion to the letter as well as the spirit of great music', the kind of claim that naturally increased Toscanini's vulnerability when he did occasionally deviate from the letter. Other conductors might be forgiven or even praised for some imaginative departure, but hardly Toscanini, even when the exception proved the rule. I remember a Beecham admirer assailing Toscanini vigorously for cutting short a sustained wind-chord at the end of the Feast of the Capulets in Berlioz's *Romeo and Juliet;* but when Beecham decided to play a passage *pizzicato* instead of *arco* in a Haydn symphony he exclaimed delightedly: 'How Haydn would have loved it!'

Beecham, like Weingartner, managed to write his autobiography *A Mingled Chime* without a single reference to Toscanini's name. Instead he spent two paragraphs blaming Verdi's music for his own lack of success in getting *Falstaff* into the English repertory: 'It is wanting in tunes of a broad and impressive character . . . the harmonic side has less variety than we find in *Otello* or the *Requiem*' and so forth. When he took pains elsewhere to refer to Leopoldo Mugnone 'whose interpretations of Verdi I have always preferred to those of any other maestro known to me, past or present', the inference by omission seemed clear enough. Cardus recalled Beecham's feeble remark that

With The NBC Symphony Orchestra at Dallas, 1st May 1950.

Toscanini was not only half-blind but stone-deaf, though such inverted hyperboles are usually disguises of pique or a grudging admiration. It is fair to add that Toscanini was as capable of intolerance as his most notorious colleagues. Menuhin reported an occasion of his 'pettiness' when he demolished a whole series of eminent conductors including the 'sentimental' Bruno Walter; but such private or semi-private tirades were probably regretted by himself more than anyone. As with many other famous performers the outward behaviour, whether Toscanini's intolerance or Beecham's facetiousness, was a self-protective veneer not to be taken at face value. 'I say terrible things about other conductors' Toscanini had told Dame Myra Hess, but on the subject of the Ninth Symphony he said to Robert Shaw:[34]

> 'You know, I have never had a good performance of this work. Sometimes the chorus is bad; sometimes the orchestra is bad; many times the soloists are bad. And many times *I* am terrible.'

Not all press-notices could be taken literally, however. *The Musical Times* quoted a choice example from a German paper during Toscanini's tour with the New York Philharmonic-Symphony:[35]

Toscanini has just given the first and last Beethoven Symphony in Berlin, and when his men laid down their instruments, the audience sobbed for quarter of an hour.

'Believe that who will!' was Percy Scholes's comment in *The Mirror of Music*, especially since neither of those works was played on the tour. Such inflated journalese followed in the wake of more serious criticism throughout most of Toscanini's career and it could work in the reverse direction too. After the famous cancellation of *Norma* during his first period at La Scala, a Milan critic called Pompeo Ferrari wrote:[36]

> Who could not have foreseen that La Scala would be made the laughing-stock of Art under the sceptre of that little king who answers to the name of Maestro Toscanini? – a man who has built his fame upon the absolute ignorance of every form of politeness. . . .

Was this the same Toscanini that Puccini praised for 'making La Scala into a real temple for artistic consecrations and re-consecrations'?

★　　★　　★　　★　　★

Criticism of Toscanini, whether as man or musician, has always thrived on such extremes; and a good deal of popular journalism, including books like Chotzinoff's and Taubman's, revolved round anecdotes of his foibles and eccentricities: his 'difficult' temperament, his rehearsal tantrums, his childish obsessions and his culinary fads. Maybe it was necessary as a kind of safety-valve for him to have relays of spare batons to break or cheap watches to stamp on, and it was certainly useful for his hosts to know that he liked champagne but not caviare, or enjoyed the company of attractive women but strongly disapproved of divorce. The trouble is that strings of such anecdotes, like collections of Beecham stories, give a misleadingly one-sided picture of a great man who was known to his friends as a person of integrity and wide cultural interests. He had, for example, a passion for the visual arts. The parallel between painting and music often struck him, as it did his friend the artist Vittore Grubicy who wrote to him: 'To me, the colours and shapes of a scene represent musical values, now simple melodic waves, now harmonic chords, rich in polyphony, but with every note distinguishable.' Those last words, coming from a pointillist painter, must have appealed to Toscanini with his passion for clarity in polyphony. As for the conflict in his own personality, Friedelind Wagner, whom he befriended after her father Siegfried's death and helped to get to America during the Hitler war, said: 'I have yet to meet a great artist whose character is as wonderful as his artistry – except when his name is Toscanini.'

Stories of Toscanini's kindness and tolerance were less likely to hit the headlines. One concerned a wind-player in the BBC Orchestra who insulted him at rehearsal after they had encountered difficulties with a particular passage. When apologies were made for him afterwards Toscanini brushed them aside and said sadly: 'Perhaps it is not his fault; people sometimes reach the stage when they are no longer able to care.' It was Toscanini's own degree of caring, his *concern* for the way the music was played, that made his life worth living. In this respect his vitality in old age was staggering enough. It was not simply a freak of stamina or temperament: it was the vitality of mind and heart, and above all that of ear, ear for the smallest detail and ear for a work as a whole. Add his phenomenal powers of concentration and communication and we have some of the ingredients that, in the opinions of many, placed him in a class of his own. But the quality of 'caring' crowned them all. It affected a rehearsal just as much as a concert: music was being made, and the presence or absence of an audience did not change the responsibility.

This helps to explain his own self-effacing manner before the public, which reminded Helen Henschel of her father Sir George Henschel:[37]

> The same quick, purposeful walk on to the platform, the same direct approach to the work, the same economy of gesture, even the same little characteristics, such as sometimes keeping the left hand on the coat lapel or the hip during straightforward passages. . . . And, above all, the same almost deprecatory manner of acknowledging applause by a little upward wave of the hands.

Applause in fact not only embarrassed Toscanini but gave him physical pain, as he explained to the American journalist Max Smith during his days at the Metropolitan: 'It is an instinct. I had the feeling as a boy when I played the cello for the first time in public. As soon as the hand-clapping began I could not resist the impulse to rush into hiding. . . .' Unlike other applause-seeking virtuosos Toscanini never willingly took a bow by himself, as Sir Adrian Boult recalled after the first of the Philharmonia concerts in 1952:[38]

> It was indeed only because the orchestra at the end resolutely refused to rise that we were able, with them, to express our deep appreciation to the Maestro himself.

Nostalgia obviously plays a part with older generations. There was nothing quite like the anticipatory excitement of a Toscanini concert or more touching than his own complete absorption in the music.

'Toscanini has given us again and again this sense of absorbed and self-forgetful dedication' wrote Lawrence Gilman, whose book *Toscanini and Great Music* appeared in the early days of the NBC broadcasts from New York. Mr Gilman was writing in gratitude and appreciation and was entirely eulogistic. On the subject of the *melos*, the melodic principle, in Wagner he said:[39]

Yet Toscanini reminds us that song and drama interpenetrate; and his own excelling gift is that of blending beauty with vitality, loveliness with strength. He is the unapproachable magician of orchestra song: yet there is no such master of rhythm, of heroic and dramatic evocation; no such architect of climax: his crescendi shake the spirit by their inexorable sweep and power and momentum.

Such hyperboles could hardly have been surpassed in the full flood of the Romantic period but should not be confused with uncritical worship. Mr Gilman, as an admired and experienced critic, wrote in general terms about Toscanini's undeniably unique qualities. Others could have quite severe strictures even over his beloved Verdi. When the controversial recording of *La Traviata* was issued *The Record Guide* suggested that the border-line between triumph and tyranny was a tenuous one:[40]

> Toscanini's reading of the score must in any case retain a permanent historic interest, though we hope it will not in future generations be regarded as the authentic Verdian gospel which it ought by rights to have been. . . . In the process of defeating the tyranny of singers Toscanini has developed a still more rigid tyranny of his own.

But when *Otello* appeared, the same writers said:[41]

> His handling of the score holds the listener enthralled, and he has evidently inspired the brilliant chorus and orchestra as well as his three principal singers to excel themselves.

The border-line, as in all artistic judgments, was however dependent to some extent on the conditioning and orientation of the listener: personal taste is seldom free from prejudice and tradition.

In any case Toscanini was his own severest critic. Taubman recalled two occasions when he turned aside compliments on a good performance with remarks such as 'Not true, it wasn't!' or 'So you think I don't know music?' Nevertheless his taste and judgment were often queried: how he could pass this recording and not that, or play Bach-Respighi so repeatedly to the neglect of original Bach, or make out-of-style adjustments in scoring to classical works, or build programmes with such bizarre juxtapositions. Many music-lovers would give years of their lives to be able to experience or re-experience the *Eroica* or the Verdi *Requiem* from Toscanini in the flesh, though few would choose to listen a second time to his recording of the Mozart E flat Symphony, K543.

Posterity has already shown a sufficiently lasting interest in Toscanini for sleuths to set about compiling statistics of his performances. Quite a few critics attacked the limitations of his repertory: his scant attention to Bach, to Mozart's operas, or to important twentieth-century composers. It is true that he played no Bartók, Hindemith or Schoenberg and only a modicum of early

Stravinsky; and that for many years he wasted time on a good deal of third-rate music. It must be stressed again however that he championed a vast amount of 'new' music of his own generation including such varied orchestral works as *En Saga, La Mer, Till Eulenspiegel* and the *Enigma* Variations. Yet for almost two-thirds of his sixty-eight active conducting years he was in his own words 'a man of the theatre'. By the time he left La Scala in 1929 he had directed no less than 117 different operas, given world premières of many of them, and introduced many more to Italy or America, ranging from *Boris* and *Eugene Onegin* to *Pelléas* and *Ariane et Barbe-bleue*. In fact his repertory, operatic and orchestra, was formidable enough to demolish any patronising complaints about 'the same old programme' and if he did tend to over-play certain favourite works in his later years he was not the only conductor to do so. As for the contemporary cause he admired Mitropoulos for being able to memorise scores like *Wozzeck* and *Lulu* but had neither the desire nor the ability to compete in music that was not 'part of his spirit'.

His repertory however did encompass a curious collection of twentieth-century works. Between the wars he took in his stride (and of course in his memory) such modernish 'effect pieces' as Honegger's *Pacific 231* and

Relaxing at San Francisco during the 1950 NBC tour.

Mossolov's *Iron Foundry,* neither of which he revived in his NBC years. It is surprising too how many larger-scale works he prepared for a solitary performance, like Roy Harris's Third Symphony or Kurt Atterberg's Sixth, which had won the Schubert Centenary prize for a new symphony in 1928. Toscanini played it with the NBC in 1943 and with staggering brilliance and popular success, but he never repeated it. Sibelius, on the other hand, had been 'part of his spirit' since the turn of the century, though he only performed *En Saga* and *The Swan* with any regularity. Yet he was a marvellous advocate for the Second Symphony and even more so for the enigmatic Fourth – which he considered one of the greatest works of its time. One longed in fact to hear that incomparable grasp of structure and control of texture at work on the Fifth and Seventh symphonies with their subtly calculated tempo-changes, but he touched neither. Sometimes a single interpretative problem could keep him away from a work he otherwise admired. He might be convinced by a light-weight or trivial piece and play it for far more than it was worth, and yet remain aloof from an accepted masterpiece or near-masterpiece. It was not a question of style. For example, he loved Bellini's *Norma* and was ideally suited to conduct it; but the casting of the title-part troubled him and he never returned to it after the fiasco in his early days at La Scala. Nor, despite his special feeling for Berlioz, did he ever perform the *Symphonie Fantastique.* Somehow and somewhere he played the last two movements only, but he was unconvinced by the harmonic and formal manoeuvres of the first and third for all their obvious genius; though it was one of many works he constantly re-studied and he even contemplated conducting it at the time of his retirement.

Statistics of the Toscanini repertory have always been hard to compile owing to the vast ramifications of his earlier career and his own indifference to such research. Meanwhile his posthumous reputation rests more and more squarely on recordings, commercial and otherwise. They cannot tell the whole story, however vividly they may convey parts of it. Out of a hundred and seventeen different operas only seven, or at most nine, have come down to us complete. There are one or two isolated acts and a few extended extracts, but no *Boris,* no *Turandot,* no *Pelléas.* The orchestra repertory was more systematically surveyed but most of it at a very late stage indeed. In the nineteen-fifties, just before and just after Toscanini's death, two writers analysed this recorded legacy in some detail. Robert C Marsh in *Toscanini and the Art of Orchestral Performance* (1956) based his findings on the records issued up to that time and on Toscanini's American and British appearances from 1926 onwards, including the tours with the Philharmonic-Symphony and the NBC. The conclusions he drew from his statistics lost validity by the exclusion of Toscanini's many guest engagements elsewhere, whether Vienna, Salzburg, Palestine or Philadelphia, Paris or Lucerne, even the post-war Scala concerts. Dr Marsh wrote out of great veneration for his subject but was outspoken to a degree of flippancy about his later tendencies:[42]

Toscanini acknowledges the applause of a packed house at La Scala Milan, at the close of a Wagner concert given on 19th September 1952.

> The defects of Toscanini come from characteristics desirable in the mean being carried to excess. His rhythmic accuracy is splendid, but at times it has been metronomic rather than musical and the performance has revealed mechanical exactitude rather than a feeling of creativity and sponteneity. His intensity is magnificent, but on occasion it has gone beyond reasonable limits. . . . Another of Toscanini's weaknesses is a tendency, like Koussevitsky's, to over-refine music which he plays too frequently. . . . The musician must always balance himself between seemingly opposite poles: the achievement of near-perfection in polish and form at the cost of losing communicative and expressive power. With Toscanini the first extreme – near-perfection – was the reef on which lay the shattered hulks of several of his most-performed works. . . .

However exaggerated this may sound, it is at least more reasoned and constructive than the Canadian pianist Glenn Gould's dismissal of Toscanini's performances in general as a 'metronomised steeple-chase'. Dr Marsh is interesting too on the subject of Toscanini's 'changing artistry' with special reference to German music:[43]

> Three 'performances' can be distinguished. First the 'ancestral' performance, that is, the earliest Toscanini performance of a German work, based upon his assimilation of the reading of German conductors;

secondly, the 'transitional' performance, in which Toscanini's *bel canto* manner has replaced some of the German style and rhetorical devices have been subdued; third, the 'singing' performance, in which German influences have disappeared and Toscanini has reconceived the work in terms of little or no rhetoric.

The influence of German conductors on Toscanini's early performances is conjectural and most unlikely. It is improbable that he heard anyone conduct *Götterdämmerung* or the Brahms Tragic Overture or the Schubert C major Symphony before he introduced them in his first season at Turin in 1895-6. As with other artists of the pre-radio age, and like Haydn at Esterházy, he 'was forced to be original'. He did not hear a German production of Wagner until 1899. Steinbach's Brahms performances with the Meiningen orchestra impressed him greatly, but that was ten years later still.

Spike Hughes in *The Toscanini Legacy* (1959) dealt with the recordings more informally and drew on his many memories of live performances and rehearsals by way of comparison. I always felt it a pity that having devoted nearly a hundred pages to Beethoven and well over a hundred to Verdi Mr Hughes' personal tastes and allergies should lead him to dispose of Brahms in two pages and Wagner in four, since both composers were so important to Toscanini and indeed to the legacy. Two recurring phrases in his commentary were however happily chosen and applicable to everything Toscanini conducted: his ability to achieve 'matching dynamics' in conversational passages between wind and strings, one of the great secrets of his control of texture; and his uncanny gift of bringing to life, and to light, 'what is there'. This must be an eternal rondo-theme in any discussion of Toscanini – as it has been in the present book – and Mr Hughes returned to it over the 'trial scene' at the end of Strauss's *Till Eulenspiegel*, where a broadening of tempo took him by surprise:[44]

> Why, of all the conductors I have ever heard conduct *Till Eulenspiegel* it should have been an Italian who first made me take note of the composer's words 'etwas breiter' at that point, I cannot imagine. But that was one's experience with Toscanini time and again. He saw what was there, no matter what language it was written in.

Spike Hughes ended his preface with the obvious enough statement that 'there will never be another Arturo Toscanini'. Yet one is tempted to add: 'Nor another comparable with him'. History and circumstances do not repeat themselves, and the age of the untrammelled ear and the divine autocrat has passed away, which does not preclude or prejudice the advent of quite different types of musical genius.

The words 'divine autocrat' are gleaned from the novelist Marcia Davenport, whose mother Alma Gluck had sung The Happy Shade in Gluck's *Orfeo* with Toscanini in 1909 at the Metropolitan. Her tributes and memories naturally concentrate on his operatic achievements. Opera-lovers too young to have heard Toscanini in person may still 'find out what all the fuss is about' from the recordings:[45]

Sheer listening answers the question of what Toscanini was and what he did. Listen to the first act of *Falstaff*, the second act of *Aida*, the third act of *La Traviata*, the Prisoners' Chorus and the second act of *Fidelio*, the second act of *Un Ballo in Maschera*. . . . these hold the answers to the question that can only be answered by the Maestro himself. In his immortality he lives on to answer it with music as it never sounded at any time, or in any hands, before or since.

As a close friend of the Toscanini family Marcia Davenport attended many of his rehearsals including the historic one of *Meistersinger* at Salzburg in 1936 which, as she described it, 'went without a flaw from beginning to end':[46]

We who heard that rehearsal – and saw it, because the memory of Maestro in his black cassock-like rehearsal coat with the light on his face remains as vivid as on that day – were overwhelmed with emotion. But when the curtain fell on the finale, and then went up again as curtains do at rehearsals for technical reasons, there stood the entire company on stage, every one of them in tears. Maestro himself stood motionless in his place with his right hand covering his eyes.

Those who had similar experiences at Toscanini rehearsals will know that this is not a novelist's flight of invention. The participants themselves are not prone to exaggerate such matters: Lotte Lehmann was the Eva, and Hans Hermann Nissen the Sachs. Nissen, according to Lehmann, had a rather phlegmatic disposition and was not easily carried away by emotions or nervous crises. Yet she too recalled:[47]

Even this man was stirred to his very depths by the great Maestro. I can still see him, his eyes overflowing with tears, as he turned around after the 'Wach auf' chorus in the general rehearsal, saying: 'My God, how shall I be able to sing now? This damned demon down there has absolutely devastated me with his fire.'

This was fulfilling Wagner's own purpose with a vengeance, since in the opera Sachs *should* in fact be overcome by the spontaneous outburst of homage from the crowd. It may be felt a little ironic that some of Toscanini's rehearsals, especially the final ones, surpassed the actual performances; but there was no question of 'saving something' for the performance – one made music from one's whole being regardless of the public. Dame Myra Hess, after hearing such a rehearsal in New York, said she was so moved that she wished the entire musical world had been there. Then, on second thoughts, she reflected more metaphysically that the fact of such sounds going out into the atmosphere, whether heard or overheard or not, could only benefit and enrich the earth.

This may seem a subjective note, even a partisan one, on which to draw a chapter on Toscanini criticism to a close. Or, taking the chapter as a whole, has the balance of pros and cons now been restored – in view of the overwhelming nature of the subject? When Toscanini first conducted the BBC Orchestra in 1935 William McNaught in *The Musical Times* took a more coolly reasoned and objective approach, but still betrayed a similar wonderment at the total effect of Toscanini's own so-called 'objectivity': [48]

> The text is enlivened from within by a complicated process for which the recipe 'play according to the composer' is but a clearing for action. No formula, however subtly applied, will give a cue for the number of new lights and new angles that continually put revealing aspects upon the familiar music, and which nevertheless came within the principle of presenting the facts.

Chapter Nine

POSTSCRIPT

When Toscanini approached the final climax of a great symphonic movement he seemed to call up unsuspected reserves of energy. It might have been the first movement of the *Eroica,* the finale of the Seventh or the coda of the Third *Leonore:* or the great build-ups at the end of the Brahms First or the Sibelius Second. In all these cases the listener had the impression of being lifted bodily from his seat in the hall. One of Toscanini's fears in his later years was that he would no longer be able to summon the strength 'to bring the big fortissimo up from the ground'. No orchestra, it seems, could produce and control such an effect through its own collective volition, though the NBC players gave a fair imitation of some of the outward aspects of a Toscanini performance when they gave a concert without a conductor as a tribute to him after his retirement. But the extra 'something' came from within. It was a quality Toscanini never took for granted in himself, one compounded of alertness of mind, keenness of ear, eternal anxiety and a kind of religious fervour. A photograph was taken of Toscanini and some of his players listening to a play-back during a recording session. Everyone is smiling and relaxed – except for him. The look of apprehension and concentration tells its own story. What was he listening for, apart from material perfection? Lotte Lehmann once asked him at a rehearsal: 'Won't you please tell us *what* you want?' He replied: 'There is no fire. . . .' On another occasion he made his much-quoted appeal to the NBC Orchestra: 'No sleep when you play! Every note – entusiasmo – like me! I am sorry, I don't enjoy to conduct, no, I hate to conduct, I hate, because I suffer too much. You look at me like you are sorry – you believe I am crazy? No, no – sensitive, yes – don't look at me in this way! Da capo!'

So the communication of enthusiasm – call it love or fervour – was an essential part of the secret. The enthusiasm, amounting to a religion, was for the music itself, for the mind of the composer. It must infect every player, every singer and every note. Without this quality the most astonishing control, the miraculous clarity and the architectural certainty would remain, as it were, uninhabited. It was the total sum that so often left Toscanini's listeners enriched but baffled – and his performers too. The cellist Willem de Mont told how he went with some other well-seasoned players for their usual pint at the 'Gluepot', the pub round the corner from the Queen's Hall, after Toscanini had conducted the *Missa Solemnis* with the BBC Orchestra. They

Backstage at the Carnegie Hall on 22nd November 1953 with Nicolas Moldovan and Carlton Cooley, members of the viola section of The NBC Symphony Orchestra.

lifted their glasses several times and put them down again without drinking and without speaking, until one of them said: 'What have we just done?'

'Toscanini delights in *fortissimi*' wrote T W Gervais 'but there is always the sense of a still further reserve. Moreover, in the most exciting *fortissimo* the music still sings.' The words 'cantando' and 'cantare' linger in the minds of those who heard him rehearse: 'sing, always sing – even when you are counting your rests!', as Sir Adrian Boult recalled him saying. But this also affected the other extreme of dynamics: the inaudible *pianissimo* was not in Toscanini's musical vocabulary. He learnt early on from Verdi on the orchestra's need to 'sing' even at the quietest levels, but at no level did he ever indulge in effect for effect's sake. A comparison with his well-known compatriot, the conductor Victor de Sabata, over one small point in Verdi's *Otello* makes this clear and might be multiplied a thousandfold. In the last act the ethereal postlude to Desdemona's 'Ave Maria' is followed by the quiet but sinister entry of the double-basses signifying the stealthy arrival of Otello. How tempting to underline this with some special interpretative effect, a comma or an accent, or both – which is just how De Sabata played it when he brought the Scala company to London. Toscanini in his recording rejected any such method, indulged in no tricks, took Verdi's marks at face value, and achieved a result that was spine-chilling in its realism.

Toscanini in 1946, standing in front of his house overlooking the Hudson River.

Although Toscanini satisfied the mind as well as the emotions through such scrupulous honesty his scruples were not slavish. Cases have been mentioned of adjustments that he made here and there when he felt sincerely that a composer had miscalculated. Samuel Chotzinoff reported that Toscanini had asked him during a rehearsal of Beethoven's Eighth Symphony:[49]

> 'What would you think, *caro,* if I reinforced the orchestration of the theme in the first movement when it arrives *fff?* You know, I have not slept nights thinking to it. It is very seldom that Beethoven puts three fortes; that means he wants the theme to sound very strong. . . . But he was deaf and he never heard it played. Do you think I dare change? . . .'

This moment of recapitulation, with the theme in the bass so easily swamped by the weight of the harmony above, is notoriously hard to make clear; but Chotzinoff's story that the innovation was tried out and rejected on his advice in February 1946 is plausible but apocryphal. Toscanini did not play or rehearse the Eighth that year, though he had habitually reinforced the rhythm of the theme on the timpani for at least a decade, only discarding it in his 1952 recording. This at least testifies to his eternal freshness of mind even in old age. It is more to the point to remind posterity that he was probably the only conductor of his time to convey the full dynamic force, the drive and the vitality, implied by Beethoven's marking *Allegro vivace e con brio.*

121

Posterity, however, may ask: even if we accept the general premise that Toscanini eschewed rhetoric more and more in his later performances, were there not in fact times when his pursuit of the truth led to inflexibility and even, dare one say, insensitivity? But what do we mean by 'insensitive'? His reluctance to indulge the whim of the moment at the expense of the higher purpose of art? His readiness to fulfil, or to seek to fulfil the composer's written requests – as when, for example, Beethoven ended the *Missa Solemnis* or the *Pastoral* Symphony with an abrupt and almost impatient gesture?

The quite special reverence and affection that many of us felt for Toscanini were not simply on account of his own views and his own gifts. It was because time and time again he made us believe that the works he conducted were perfect masterpieces to which every detail contributed. The devotion he earned from his colleagues, it must be said again, was unique; though there were always a few who rejected him, as one of his players said, because they could never forgive him his greatness. It matters nothing that he could not possibly have encompassed the different conceptions of others, say of Furtwängler or Klemperer or Bruno Walter. It matters little that he sometimes fell short of his ideal, if in his own opinion he ever attained it. What then do we still learn from Toscanini? Devotion to his art and the ceaseless striving towards such an ideal of recreation. The ideal will always be changing in subtle and elusive ways but the search, as with him, may bring untold rewards in spite of its frustrations and dissatisfactions. The most important thing about Toscanini is that he made us aware of ideals and standards of involvement we should otherwise never have known.

REFERENCES

1 Harvey Sachs, *Toscanini*. London, Weidenfeld and Nicolson, 1978, pp 34-35
2 Della Corte, quoted by H Sachs, p 75
3 Howard Taubman, *The Maestro*. New York, Simon and Schuster, 1951, p 118
4 *The New York Times*, 2 January 1908
5 ibid, 14 April 1913
6 ibid, 29 December 1920
7 ibid
8 Klemperer quoted in analytical note to HMV Album 82 (Toscanini/NYP-S Haydn 'Clock')
9 *Corriere della sera*, Milan, December 1922, tr.Sachs
10 Filippo Sacchi, *The Magic Baton*. London, Putnam, 1957, p 168
11 Sachs, p 173
12 Sachs, p 199
13 B H Haggin, *The Toscanini Musicians Knew*, New York, Horizon Press, 1967, p 62
14 *The Sunday Times*, 26 November 1950
15 *The Listener*, 3 April 1952
16 Haggin, pp 154-5
17 *The Times*, 17 August 1937
18 Lawrence Gilman, *Toscanini and Great Music*, London, The Bodley Head, 1939, Intro. pp xi-xii
19 Eugene Goossens, *Overture and Beginners*
20 Michael Kennedy, *Barbirolli*, London, McGibbon and Key, 1971
21 *The Times*, 8 June 1935
22 *The Sunday Times*, 26 November 1950
23 J A Westrup, *Sharps and Flats*. London, OUP, 1940, p 199
24 Haggin, p 126
25 Bernard Shore, *The Orchestra Speaks*. London, Longmans, 1938, p 169
26 Rosenfield quoted in ATS periodical, *The Maestro*, Vol 2, 1970, p 11
27 Haggin, p 184
28 *The Times*, 25 January 1954
29 quoted in *The News Chronicle*, 8 December 1949
30 Haggin, p 83
31 Letter to DM, 5 December 1950
32 *Grove's Dictionary of Music and Musicians*, 5th ed, London, Macmillan, 1954, Vol 8, pp 518-9
33 HMV Record Review, July 1942
34 Haggin, pp 80-81
35 Percy Scholes, *The Mirror of Music*. London, Novello and OUP, 1947, p 403
36 Sachs, p 66
37 Helen Henschel, *When Soft Voices Die*. London, Westhouse, 1944, p 37
38 BBC broadcast, 1 Oct 1952
39 Gilman, p 183

40 E Sackville-West and Desmond Shawe-Taylor, *The Record Guide*. London, Collins, 1955, p 803
41 ibid, pp 809-810
42 Robert C Marsh, *Toscanini and the Art of Orchestral Performance*. London, Allen and Unwin, 1956, pp 78-9
43 ibid, p 108
44 Spike Hughes, *The Toscanini Legacy*. London, Putnam, 1959, p 210
45 *The Maestro*, Vol 1, 1969, p 6
46 Marcia Davenport, *Too Strong for Fantasy*. London, Collins, 1968, p 195
47 *The Maestro*, Vol 1, 1969, p 7
48 *The Musical Times*, July 1935
49 Samuel Chotzinoff, *Toscanini: An Intimate Portrait*. London, Hamish Hamilton, 1956, p 120

TOSCANINI
– a selected discography

During a rehearsal for the 1947 NBC broadcasts of Verdi's *Otello*, Arturo Toscanini referred the members of his orchestra to a text he had brought with him into the studio. That text mirrored, more or less exactly, Maestro's honest and dignified approach to the art of musical interpretation: those words that Shakespeare had scripted for Hamlet's speech to his players applied no less to the musical credo of this century's most noted and influential conductor. Surely Toscanini, who so often underlined the importance of being true to the composer's score, was thinking particularly of the following passage from the beginning of Act 3, Scene 2:

> '. . . anything (so) o'erdone is from the purpose of playing, whose end, both at the first and now, was and is to hold, as 'twere, the mirror up to nature; to show virtue her own feature, scorn her own image, and the very age and body of the time his form and pressure.'

Hamlet goes on to reproach those players who indulge in various interpretative excesses; sentiments that were certainly echoed frequently enough by the great conductor. Yet Toscanini was no advocate of the bloodless, 'correct' run-through: 'the score' to him was more a symbol of a work's life-blood than a succession of dots and dashes that, when strung together, just happen to mean 'music'.

A Toscanini performance could never be relegated to the realms of 'casual listening': there is too much intense concentration in his readings for that, too many relevant details that clamour for attention and too few opportunities for the listener's mind to wander! His whole approach is essentially recreative, though strengthened with a rigorous sense of discipline and a keen intellect. You will listen in vain for subjective over-indulgence or wilful distortion of a work's structure. Toscanini's detractors complain of his supposed 'rigidity', his 'tendency to speed' or his 'aggressive approach'. It would be fairer to comment on his secure rhythmic control, his refusal to let the music sag and the pulse slacken and his acknowledgement of sforzandi and strong accents where written. Those listeners who were weaned on low-key, complacent performances cannot really be blamed for over-reacting to Toscanini's assertive approach to the scores he conducted. To be fair, those positive qualities that I have just catalogued *did* occasionally slip into their negative counterparts (listed previously), but those occasions were indeed rare.

One of the most remarkable aspects of Toscanini's art is the consistency of his approach: he studied each work he performed with total commitment and rarely ventured far from the integrated interpretation he invariably achieved. If you study his recordings carefully, you will spot many small instances where a later performance differs from its predecessor in countless slightly altered nuances or dynamics, phrases marginally expanded or contracted and tempi subtly modified. You will virtually never come across a work that has been completely 're-thought'; any uncertainty or doubt as to how a piece should 'go' was surely worked out in Toscanini's study before his own first performance of the piece in question. I hasten to add that his interpretations never stagnated: they simply developed slowly, reinforcing the ground on which they were built.

If I were to sum up Toscanini's art in a single phrase, it would be 'interpretative integrity'. The price was indeed high for a Toscanini performance: as a conductor, he always gave of himself wholeheartedly to the task in hand and the men in his orchestra unfailingly gave themselves over to their maestro's vision with a degree of industry and enthusiasm that has rarely, if ever, been matched by any similar group of players. The one person who *never* paid a price was the composer: he was always the honoured guest at the proceedings. The recorded legacy that I have undertaken to introduce to my readers is indeed unique in the annals of the gramophone: we should treasure it.

Just a word about my comments on the individual discs. Space does not allow me to indulge in any sort of detailed analysis. To do justice to a Toscanini performance in terms of verbal description would be a long and fruitless task; in the end, the music itself must speak. I have therefore tried to sum up briefly the 'feel' of a performance and in so doing lead my reader to those discs that are most truly representative of Toscanini's art. I provide you with a rough guide rather than an analytical inspection, and in so doing I make grateful acknowledgement to Professor Matthews for his unfailing encouragement and advice: any errors or excesses which persist are mine, not his. My thanks are also due to Robert Cowan for checking my original draft and for his many helpful comments; to Christopher Dyment for making so freely available to me his specialist knowledge, and to Ralph Mace for his invaluable advice and for making it possible for me to hear many pressings which would not otherwise have been available to me.

In closing, I must make reference to the many 'pirated' Toscanini records that are, from time to time, available from specialist record shops and dealers. These limited issues are *not* taken from commercially recorded material and are often available only in quite atrocious sound. Nonetheless, they often enshrine performances that are central to a full understanding of Maestro's art. I must urge readers to investigate these issues for themselves: as a pastime, such a voyage of discovery will prove most rewarding. I would also like to point out that, although I have listened to Toscanini records on a fairly large variety of reproducing equipment*, your own room acoustics and record-playing set-up will largely dictate what *sort* of sound comes over best in your home. For instance, a transfer that is comparatively dry and lacking in resonance will sound better in a larger room; a smoother, slightly less restricted cut will sound a little kinder in a small room. Personal taste plays a great part in all this and I urge the reader to experiment for himself.

RAY BURFORD

*My own domestic equipment, in a lounge measuring 13½' by 14½', consists of a JVC JA-S77 amplifier, a Thorens TD 160B turntable fitted with an SME Series III arm and a moving-coil stereo Coral MC 81 cartridge, and a pair of Lowther Voigt Classic 115s speakers.

Abbreviations

*asterisk before the date indicates a broadcast of which a recording was made and subsequently released.

arr.	arranged by
AT	prefix for records in the RCA 'Toscanini Edition', a bargain series devoted to the re-issue of Toscanini's commercial recordings. 12″ mono lps.
BBCSO	British Broadcasting Corporation Symphony Orchestra.
DaCa	Da Capo. Prefix for German EMI 12″ mono bargain lp.
EMI	Electrical Musical Industries.
Eng.	English release.
Fr.	French release.
Ger.	German release.
HMV	His Masters Voice (EMI).
It.	Italian release.
JAP	Series of 100 12″ mono lps issued in Japan only (by Victor) containing all the commercially released recordings Toscanini made for Victor.
LM	Prefix for 12″ mono Victor lp.
NBC	National Broadcasting Company (of America).
NCRA	No commercial recording availablle.
NY Phil-Sym.	New York Philharmonic-Symphony Orchestra.
Phil. Academy	Academy of Music, Philadelphia.
Orch.	Orchestra.
RCA	Radio Corporation of America.
VCM/VIC	Prefix for Victrola, a 12″ mono bargain Victor lp.
VICS	as above, but simulated stereo.
WRC	World Record Club.

A Selected Discography

BACH, Johann Sebastian

Suite No.3 in D: Air

8 April 1946
NBC
Carnegie Hall
NCRA

In spite of his scant attention to Bach, the Air was surely a 'must' for Toscanini, lending itself to his unerring feeling for line. He naturally plays it in the original key and not in Wilhelmj's once-popular but unauthentic version for the G string. In its more celestial register the Air reveals the serenity and simplicity that only great art can achieve, and the subtly varied string texture produces effects of extraordinary beauty.

BARBER, Samuel

Adagio for Strings

19 March 1942
NBC
Carnegie Hall
NCRA

This Adagio is drawn from the composer's String Quartet op 11. Toscanini gave the world première on 5 November 1938 in a programme that also included Barber's first Essay for orchestra. The recorded version is still unsurpassed, superbly proportioned with a beautifully achieved climax and an affecting coda: in fact, a model of exact pacing.

BEETHOVEN, Ludwig van

Piano Concerto no 1 in C, op 15
(soloist: Ania Dorfman)

9 August 1945
NBC
Carnegie Hall
RCA AT 106
Amer/RCA VIC 1521

Dorfman's playing is accomplished and sometimes more. As with most of Toscanini's concerto recordings the striking feature is the accompaniment, full of illuminating detail and rhythmically alert. The English AT 106 has an honest, clean sound and is cut on a single side. The JAP is fine, but it is worth making an effort to acquire the VIC 1521. This pressing has the third movement at the start of side 2 – but what a difference! The fill-up is the 1939 version of the Overture *Leonore no 3* in superb sound.

Piano Concerto no 3 in C minor, op 37
(soloist: Arthur Rubinstein)

*29 October 1944
NBC
Studio 8H
It/RCA RL 42860

Although Rubinstein's accustomed style seems at variance with the conductor's severely classical approach, Toscanini showed great interest in having this part of the broadcast concert released commercially. Nonetheless, has one ever heard the orchestral framework come alive as it does here? The JAP AT 1016 is marvellously done, and the pitch fluctuations found on LCT 1009 have been eliminated.

BEETHOVEN (cont.)

Piano Concerto no 4 in G, op 58
(soloist: Rudolf Serkin)

*26 November 1944
NBC
Studio 8H
RCA AT 106
Amer/RCA LM 2797

In the first and third concertos the fervour and the excitement had to be generated mainly by the orchestra, but here we have a great and more equal partnership. Serkin had played this work with Toscanini, along with Mozart's K595, at his American debut in 1936. Preparation and understanding are evident in every bar. AT 106 is good, with clean piano and orchestral sound, and the JAP AT 1016 is excellent.

Violin Concerto in D, op 61
(soloist: Jascha Heifetz)

11 March 1940
NBC
Studio 8H
Eng/DPS 2006 (2)
Heifetz RCA Edition

Toscanini included this work in his farewell concert with the New York Philharmonic-Symphony Orchestra on 29 April 1936. Heifetz was also the soloist in the recording made with the NBC four years later. Many have paid tribute to his technical prowess at the expense of his more than considerable musicianship, but his reading of the solo part shows that subtlety as well as polish could be achieved with the right conductor. The G minor section in the first movement is not drawn out unconscionably, as so often happens, but fits structurally into a movement that is, after all, marked not *andante* but *allegro ma non troppo*. It can hardly have been Beethoven's intention to treat this as a 'slow' movement, and Toscanini's strong and vital accompaniment reveals details that usually go for nothing.

The JAP AT 1017 edition is splendid, the transfer clean, resonant and almost a complete 'face-lift' of the original recording. Compared with this the English stereo version is a sad disappointment. On the other hand, the American issue to be found in the complete Heifetz Edition is also excellent.

Overture: Consecration of the House, op 124

16 December 1947
NBC
Studio 8H
Ger/It AT 136
Amer/RCA VIC 8000 (8)

A magnificent performance of a late and ceremonial work incorporating vigorous fugal writing that may reflect Beethoven's admiration for Handel. Splendid details are also apparent in the introduction: rich brass and timpani at the *un poco più vivace* section, in which the bassoons seem to 'chase' the procession. B H Haggin reports that Toscanini once returned from a rehearsal complaining desperately that 'we try everything but we still cannot hear those bassoons'. We certainly hear them in this performance. Resonance has been added to this recording and various doctored editions have also been released. The German AT is good, but the one in VIC 8000 has the most natural sound.

Overture: Leonore no 1, op 138

1 June 1939
BBCSO
Queen's Hall
Ger/DaCa 027 01 0135
Amer/Seraphim 6015(3)

This performance of the most neglected of the *Leonore* overtures reveals many details of the score glossed over by other conductors. The BBC Symphony Orchestra played magnificently for Toscanini and he found it a responsive and well-integrated ensemble. (The sight-reading of British players always amazed him!). In a broadcast Alex Nifosi, former cellist of the BBC Symphony, spoke of the difficult string and woodwind figures in bars 12 to 22 which are so perfectly executed here.

Overture: Leonore no 2, op 72a

*25 November 1939
NBC
Studio 8H
NCRA

This recording has never been commercially available in the USA. The JAP/AT is a worthy transfer, for the 78s were not good. The performance is suitably powerful with plenty of expansion in the quieter and more relaxed passages, recalling the remarkable Beethoven cycle that Toscanini conducted with the NBC in 1939.

Overture: Leonore no 3, op 72a

*4 November 1939
NBC
Studio 8H
Amer/VIC 1521
Ger/It AT 136

Tovey's analysis of this great masterwork and his comparison between *no 3* and *no 2* make essential reading.
The last pages are so overwhelming that they leave one exhausted. Karl Glassman's timpani-roll at the end has not been matched on any other recording. In fact – to quote a well-known writer – 'no man with a heart condition should listen to this: the excitement could prove *too* much'.
VIC 1521 is magnificent and the Japanese equivalent issue almost as good. When the transfers are compared with the original English 78s one can only feel eternally grateful to the engineer who made it all possible. So many accepted performances today, with their plushly upholstered textures, give rise to a certain apprehension about the way in which future generations will 'understand' Beethoven's orchestra – for surely a degree of ruggedness is all part of his sound?

1 June 1945
NBC
Carnegie Hall
Amer/RCA LM 6025(2)

As with *Egmont*, it proved not possible to duplicate such excitement and frisson in the studio. This was the recording substituted in the complete *Fidelio*, since the one traditionally included in the broadcast of the opera proved technically unsatisfactory.

Overture: Coriolan, op 62

1 June 1945
NBC
Carnegie Hall
Catalogue numbers as above

Toscanini was insistent that Beethoven's marking of *allegro con brio* applied to the whole overture, and when Willem Mengelberg lectured him on how to play it, saying that he had his ideas from someone who knew someone etc, etc, the Maestro replied in typical fashion: 'I get my ideas from Beethoven – the score!' To those who find the second subject uncomfortable when

130

not slightly retarded it may be remarked that it is the consistent undercurrent of quavers that binds the work together.

Overture: Prometheus, op 43

18 December 1944
NBC
Studio 8H
Catalogue numbers
as above

Under Toscanini's baton this work takes on a stature which most other conductors fail to reveal in interpretations which, by comparison, seem lightweight and almost casual. With Toscanini the opening pages have weight, propulsion and superbly regulated dynamics, and the *Allegro* conveys a real sense of enjoyment. Most editions sound well.

Overture: Egmont, op 84

*18 November 1939
NBC
Studio 8H
NCRA

A performance of unparelleled splendour with hair-raising timpani and trumpet crescendi in the coda. Many recorded performances have been praised by various critics, but this one seems to offer a different piece of music. The NBC Orchestra in 1939 was not as responsive as it became in later years, but it produced playing of great power and enthusiasm, if not the last word in polish and refinement. The JAP transfer is magnificent.

19 January 1953
NBC
Carnegie Hall
Ger/It AT 136
Amer/RCA VIC 8000 (8)

In 1953 even Toscanini could not *quite* recapture the incredible fire and power of the 1939 performance, but this remains an essential disc and sounds excellent in all editions.

Fidelio, op 72b

*10 and
17 December 1944
NBC
Studio 8H
Amer/RCA LM 6025 (2)
Ger/It AT 204

When Toscanini gave his NBC broadcasts of *Fidelio* in 1944 New York had not heard him conduct a complete opera since he left the 'Met' 29 years before. It had to be something special, and the war situation made *Fidelio*, with its ethical and moral principles and its triumph of good over evil, the ideal choice. The Maestro's opposition to all forms of tyranny is a matter of public record (he and his wife Carla suffered physical injury at the hands of Fascist thugs in 1931), and Toscanini said himself that he was 'an autocrat in music but a democrat in all else'. This anti-authoritarian attitude towards politics gave *Fidelio* a special significance for him, and his pre-war Salzburg performances are still spoken of with excitement and reverence.

For many this is the greatest performance on record. The cast adapts well to Toscanini's concept: listen, for example, to the beginning of the great quartet *Mir ist so wunderbar* for its atmosphere and perfect pacing. It has been said that there are people who like music and those who like opera: this is for the first group.

Missa Solemnis, op 123

30, 31 March and
2 April 1953
NBC
Carnegie Hall
Eng/Ger/It AT 200(2)
Amer/RCA LM 6013(2)

The massive, dramatic and incandescent nature of this performance epitomises Robert C Marsh's description of the contrast between Toscanini's conducting and that of most others as 'the difference between St. Francis of Assisi in ecstasy and a priest sleepily speaking the daily office'.

Space precludes a detailed discussion of this magnificent recording though mention must be made of the end of the *Gloria*, the impact of the *Et Resurrexit*, the violin solo in the *Benedictus* and the orchestral sections of the *Agnus Dei*. In fact, the muscular and vividly clear orchestral texture provides a firm foundation for an interpretation that has unfailing continuity and finds tempi that unify and relate the various movements.

Quartet in F, op 135: Lento and Vivace

8 March 1938
NBC
Studio 8H
Ger/It AT 144
Amer/VIC 8000(8)

Beethoven's last quartets were Toscanini's musical bible and he played occasional movements from them on full orchestral strings. For listeners who were wary of the label 'chamber music' he was doing a propaganda exercise, although those deeply attached to the intimacy of the original medium might well feel uncomfortable about the result.

Septet, op 20

26 November 1951
NBC
Carnegie Hall
*Catalogue numbers
as above*

This is played with textures delicately scaled down to preserve the correct proportion of strings and wind. The inflections are those of a chamber ensemble such as Adolf Busch achieved with his Chamber Players in the 1930s in, for example, Mozart's *Serenata Notturna*. The Septet appears stronger for the increased weight: the single-sided VIC 8000 is excellent, but needs a volume lift: the German AT on the other hand is slightly larger than life.

Symphony no 1 in C, op 21

30 March 1921
(4th movt. only)
La Scala Orch.
Camden NJ
NCRA

25 October 1937
BBCSO
Queen's Hall
Eng/WH 134 (WRC)
Amer/Seraphim 6015(3)

21 December 1951
NBC
Carnegie Hall
Eng/Ger/It AT 117
Amer/VIC 8000 (8)

Toscanini conducted Beethoven's First Symphony as far back as 1896, when he visited La Scala from Turin to give a series of concerts. His approach to the work was marked by an irresistible eagerness and vitality and by an awareness of the muscular strength inherent in the score. Its symphonic structure was enhanced by lean textures and a scrupulous avoidance of the more opulent string sound favoured by some conductors. Woodwind and brass are well to the fore, and the work is played as early Beethoven and not as late Haydn or Mozart. The old La Scala disc is not quite such a museum-piece as some would have us believe, since the orchestra was obviously a first-rate ensemble and the performance of the final movement which we hear resembles the later ones in all the essentials. Familiar details prove that once a ground-plan was established it was not likely to change, however much the structure itself might vary.

The BBC performance has broader tempi, especially in the first and last movements, but the mood and basic outlook are similar to those expressed in the later version with the NBC. Toscanini made the second movement repeat with the BBC but not in the NBC version.

Symphony no 2 in D, op 36

7 November 1949
(1st movt. only)
and 5 October 1951
NBC
Carnegie Hall
Eng/Ger/It AT 117
Amer/VIC 8000 (8)

In the first movement Toscanini and Beecham (at least in his 1957 HMV recording) are remarkably similar in their approach, but in subsequent movements they part company. Nobody reveals the young giant Beethoven flexing his muscles in preparation for the *Eroica* as Toscanini does. The slow movement can easily drag if not urged gently forward and the scherzo surely demands this dynamic impact. It is unusual that so long a period separates the first movement from the recording of the others..

Symphony no 3 in E flat, op 55 (Eroica)

*28 October 1939
NBC
Studio 8H
NCRA

28 November and
5 December 1949
NBC
Carnegie Hall
NCRA

*6 December 1953
NBC
Carnegie Hall
Eng/Ger/It AT 121
Amer/VIC 8000 (8)

The Maestro played this symphony more than any other during the course of his long career in America. All three recordings are discussed as one entry.

In spite of the revolutionary quality of the work, it is important to remember that Beethoven's orchestra only added one extra horn to that of late Haydn (as, for example in the 'London' Symphony), yet we expect in Beethoven an infinitely more powerful dynamic range. If the awaited richness and fullness of sound are to emerge from the *Eroica* it must be played with a degree of muscular power and a great sense of structure. Conductors who inflict a rag-bag of tempi on the first movement (slowing down the E minor theme in the development and so forth, with fatal loss of tension), and who turn the Funeral March into a Wagnerian catastrophe, surely have a mistaken view of the work.

Toscanini will have none of this, of course. He carries the first movement through in seemingly one tempo and with superhuman energy, yet with no loss of rhythmic poise and expressive quality. The slow movement is tragic but symphonic, the scherzo dances with an irresistible rhythm, and the great final movement does not disintegrate into a series of episodes, as so often happens. Until the arrival of the Japanese version of the AT edition it was not possible adequately to assess the 1939 performance. The 1953 broadcast is widely regarded as the greatest statement of the score: among the many points to note is the superb horn playing in the trio.

Symphony no 4 in B flat, op 60

4 November 1939
BBCSO
Queen's Hall

When Schumann described this work as 'a Greek goddess between two Norse giants' he planted in people's minds a feminine image which still persists. But

Eng/WH 134 (WRC)
Amer/Seraphim 6015 (3)

*3 February 1951
NBC
Carnegie Hall
Eng/Ger/It AT 123
Amer/RCA VIC 8000 (8)

a glance at the score reveals *fortes, fortissimi* and *sforzati* in abundance, as befits the successor to the *Eroica* and the forerunner to the Fifth Symphony. At the same time, the work does of course have its moments of gentleness, especially in the slow movement.

The BBC performance is a few seconds faster than that of the NBC but, paradoxically, creates a somewhat more relaxed impression. It must be said that the English AT issue is hopeless from the point of view of recorded sound: AT 600 is more natural, while VIC 8000 is excellent throughout.

23 December 1920
(4th movt. only)
La Scala Orch.
Camden NJ
NCRA

27 February,
1 and 29 March 1939
NBC
Studio 8H
NCRA

*22 March 1952
NBC
Carnegie Hall
Eng/Ger/It AT 128
Amer/RCA Vic 8000 (8)
CRMI 2494

Symphony no 5 in C minor, op 67

Since this is one of the most played of all symphonies many conductors have felt the need to stamp their interpretation on the music, especially on the first movement, which lends itself to rhetorical gestures. For Toscanini, however, it remains *allegro con brio*: he places his trust in Beethoven's instinct and in the markings of the score.

The acoustic Scala recording shows the same features as the later ones as far as the 'ground plan' goes. The 1939 reading is a great one: power harnessed to restraint, the NBC giving its all – an object lesson showing how to prevent majesty degenerating into pomposity. By 1952, however, Toscanini's approach favoured momentum, form and impact at the expense of relaxation. The JAP/AT 1015 is superb, though the 78s are worth preserving since certain takes are not entirely common to both issues. The English AT is also excellent and can be recommended as a safe buy.

21/22 October 1937
BBCSO
Queen's Hall
Eng/BBC 4001 (4)
Amer/Seraphim 6015 (3)
Fr/RCA GMI C 051 03854

14 January 1952
NBC
Carnegie Hall
Eng/Ger/It AT 133
Amer/RCA VIC 8000 (8)

Symphony no 6 in F, op 68 (Pastoral)

This is no easy-going account of the score – which is not to imply praise by default. No other Beethoven symphony presents so many traps for the unwary conductor. The first two movements, each in fully-worked sonata form, have certain characteristics in common but differ sharply in mood. The opening *Allegro*, for example, requires a strongly rhythmic impulse and its climaxes need the most careful control. The BBC performance is slightly faster, but omits the repeat in the first movement. Toscanini produces marvellous crescendi, while the two solo celli in the slow movement are, for once, entirely audible. Of how many interpretations can that be said?

9/10 April 1936
NY Phil-Sym.
Carnegie Hall
Eng/Ger/It AT 153

Symphony no 7 in A, op 92

The New York Philharmonic-Symphony disc is deservedly famous, and the fact that it is still in demand 44 years after the event proves its value as a musical and as an historical document. It has helped to shape the musical tastes of countless listeners.

9 November 1951
NBC
Carnegie Hall
Ger/It AT 140
Amer/RCA VIC 8000 (8)

How is the NBC recording different? There is a still greater insistence on clarity and articulation, and the woodwind soloists are not allowed quite so much freedom. It remains, nevertheless a very great performance. On the English AT (the 1936 version) much more could have been done: the quality deteriorates after the very first chord. The German AT edition is magnificent.

Symphony no 8 in F, op 93

17 April 1939
NBC
Studio 8H
NCRA

10 November 1952
NBC
Carnegie Hall
Ger/It AT 140
Amer/RCA VIC 8000 (8)

At the risk of repetition, it has to be said that no other conductor reveals the stature and the scope of this symphony as Toscanini does. We have all read that this is Beethoven's 'Little' Symphony: much the same has been said even about his op 135 Quartet. But the Eighth Symphony is in fact a work of great power and intensity. Listen, for example, to the development of the first movement and to whole areas of the finale.

Both these performances are similar in approach, but the 1952 recording wins hands down on technical grounds: this is clearly the version to have. It would seem that maintaining the tempo of the first movement is a major problem for most conductors: one has only to listen to Mengelberg (1940), Walter (1942) and Furtwängler (1953) to prove the point. But Toscanini is another matter entirely: one could have no better example of the Maestro's feeling for the 'correct' style.

Symphony no 9 in D minor, op 125 ('Choral')

31 March/1 April 1952
NBC
Carnegie Hall
Ger/It AT 143
Amer/RCA VIC 8000 (8)
RCA VIC 1607

It seems scarcely credible that a man of 85 could still electrify an orchestra and chorus to produce a result of such fanatical intensity and energy. Most of his younger colleagues give performances which seem almost sluggish by comparison. What could be more terrifying than Toscanini's account of the first movement? Some may feel that he takes *un poco maestoso* slightly too fast, but none can deny that this most titanic of opening statements is unleashed with a force no other conductor can match. His treatment of the scherzo is also characterised by an almost superhuman energy which, extends to the trio-section also. The playing of the orchestra combines accuracy of detail with a force so staggering that it is impossible to describe in words.

Toscanini's tempo for the slow movement is quicker than, for example, that of Klemperer, but there is great intensity in the playing, magnificently controlled by a profoundly objective attitude to the music. It is in the choral finale, however, that Toscanini rises to his greatest heights. The whole vast movement, which can so easily become episodic in other hands, unfolds as a single inspiration carrying all before it. The choral singing rises to the occasion and the solo quartet is well balanced.

135

BERLIOZ, Hector

Overture: Roman Carnival

19 January 1953
NBC
Carnegie Hall
Eng/Ger/It AT 100
Amer/RCA VIC 1244

This record alone is a tribute to the excellence of the NBC Symphony Orchestra and its wholehearted response to Toscanini's demands. The percussion in the introduction is worth studying closely with a score in hand. There is excellent sound in all editions.

The Damnation of Faust: Rakoczy March

24 December 1920
La Scala Orch.
Camden NJ
NCRA

*2 September 1945
NBC
Studio 8H
Ger/It AT 124

The March is excellently projected, with plenty of excitement well disciplined. The 1945 recording reveals much detail and preserves the balances typical of a Toscanini performance. One wonders what effect such playing would have on a present-day Prom audience? Toscanini conducted the whole work at La Scala in 1902.

Harold in Italy
(soloist: Carlton Cooley)

*29 November 1953
NBC
Carnegie Hall
Eng/Ger/It AT 112

This is a wonderfully powerful yet sensitive performance amply demonstrating Toscanini's mastery of rhythm and orchestral texture. He always insisted that the solo viola should come from the orchestra, thus ensuring a unity of approach. The rapport between Carlton Cooley, who led the violas in the NBC, and Toscanini suggests a long-term preparation hardly possible with a visiting soloist. The reflective opening is superbly balanced and the repeat later in the first movement is observed. In the Serenade the NBC woodwind are at their best, and the excitement of the finale is enhanced by Toscanini's control. Note the miraculous timing of the percussion in the coda – and compare the performances of some other conductors at this point!

Romeo and Juliet: Dramatic Symphony

(Complete)
*9 and 16 February 1947
NBC
Studio 8H
Ger/It AT 206 (2)

(Orchestral extracts)
17 February 1947
NBC
Carnegie Hall
NCRA

Queen Mab Scherzo
9 February 1942
Philadelphia Orch.

The three complete performances of October 1942 clearly showed what a wonderful, if slightly uneven, score this is. The broadcast of 1947 reveals a total sense of dedication and the Love Scene alone should dispel any idea that the Maestro conducted everything 'in the same way' (i.e. quickly!).
The unbelievable virtuosity of the *Queen Mab Scherzo* comes over with clarity and warmth. Arthur Berv, first horn of the NBC, described this experience as 'like climbing a mountain-face without a blade of grass to hold on to. But you felt safe with the Maestro: he knew what he was doing, and you gained confidence from that'.
For recorded quality the NBC version is recommended, but the Philadelphia's *Queen Mab* has its own rewards.

Phil. Academy
Eng/RL 01900 (5)

*10 November 1951
NBC
Carnegie Hall
Amer/RCA VIC 1267

BIZET, Georges

Carmen: Suite no 1

Act IV: Aragonaise
31 March 1921
La Scala Orch.
Camden NJ
NCRA

(Extracts)
5 August 1952
NBC
Carnegie Hall
Ger/It AT 124
Eng AT 109
Fr/RCA VL 4950
Amer/RCA VIC 1263

Toscanini conducted many performances of the complete opera, but the Suite is all we are left with. It is however quite breathtaking: the clarity and grace of the reading make it an exhilarating experience. The full impact of course depends on the quality of the recorded sound which, fortunately, is excellent in all editions.

L'Arlesienne: Suite no 2 (Farandole)

11 March 1921
La Scala Orch.
Camden NJ
NCRA

This brief sample makes one regret that the whole Suite was not recorded with the NBC.

BOITO, Arrigo

Mefistofele: Prologue

*14 March 1954
NBC
Carnegie Hall
Eng/Ger/It AT 131

When Toscanini returned to Italy to re-open La Scala in 1946 he ended his programme with this Prologue, which was also included in a Boito memorial concert there two years later. His long friendship with the composer gave the work a special significance for him, and he was its unrivalled interpreter. The NBC recording was made three weeks before Toscanini's retirement, but it shows no diminution of his remarkable powers.
Nicola Moscona, the bass, is excellent, and the Columbus Boychoir pure delight. The chorus and orchestra are in splendid form, with brass-playing of astonishing unanimity. The final climax defies description – again illustrating the Maestro's technique of keeping the supreme effort in reserve. Most editions are very good, but the German version is the best.

BRAHMS, Johannes

Academic Festival Overture, op 80

*6 November 1948
NBC
Studio 8H
Ger/It AT 152

Toscanini's reading of this well-loved work shows his unerring sense of balance between form and content – so vital in all Brahms. It is presented not as an end-of-term extravaganza of student songs, but as a classical sonata-form structure, full of strength and dignity.

Tragic Overture, op 81

25 October 1937
BBCSO
Queen's Hall
Ger/DaCa 027 01 035

*22 November 1953
NBC
Carnegie Hall
Ger/It AT 152

It is fascinating to compare these two recordings because they show how Toscanini was capable of changing his view of interpretation with the passage of time. A note of the relative playing times is instructive – 12 minutes 25 seconds for the BBC recording in 1937, and 13 minutes 45 seconds with the NBC in 1953. Yet he was often accused of playing works faster in his old age. The BBC performance has drive, pace and impact: the middle section (played more slowly than usual, but strictly in accordance with Brahms's instructions) has a poise which exemplifies once again Toscanini's unerring sense of rhythm.

The German Da Capo version is a truly remarkable example of a successful transfer from 78s to LP. The much later 1953 NBC broadcast is, perhaps, more dignified and lyrical in performance, with no loss of intensity even in the quieter sections. The voicing is different, with the brass very much to the fore: Toscanini made slight adjustments to the trumpet parts to achieve greater clarity. The German AT version of this recording is first-class.

Song of the Fates, op 89

*27 November 1948
NBC
Studio 8H
Eng/Ger/It AT 125

What an opening! Could any German conductor have extracted more menace, more power, or darker colouring from this music? Throughout the performance we hear how the NBC could transform itself into a German-sounding orchestra at Toscanini's wish. The Robert Shaw Chorale sing with conviction and power: all editions are excellent.

Hungarian Dances nos 1, 17, 20, 21 (arr. Dvorak)

17 February 1953
NBC
Carnegie Hall
Ger/It AT 118

Toscanini played the Dances with an élan and finish rarely accorded to this kind of music. At the same time it can be argued that the traditional, idiomatic gipsy accent in pacing and phrasing is somewhat lacking.

Liebeslieder Waltzes, op 52
(piano duet: Kahn and Balsam)

*13 November 1948
NBC
Studio 8H
NCRA

We normally hear the *Liebeslieder* sung by solo voices with piano duet, but Toscanini – perhaps fearing that rivalry between soloists might destroy unity – always used a chorus. The recording is good.

Piano Concerto no 2 in B flat, op 83

(soloist: Vladimir Horowitz)

9 May 1940
NBC
Carnegie Hall
Eng/Ger/It AT 103

Reservations about Horowitz as an interpreter of the great German classics do not alter the fact that he is a pianist in a million. The excitement and the range of his playing dwarf most of his rivals.

Toscanini is almost entirely with him, and the few small lapses in ensemble seem unimportant when there is so much conviction elsewhere in the performance. The balance between the solo cello and the other strings at the opening of the slow movement, and the tempo-relationship of the coda in the finale are among Toscanini's own revelations. He conducted the work in 1936 with Robert Casadesus as the pianist – an unusual partnership – but Horowitz was the soloist in all later performances.

Double Concerto in A minor, op 102

(soloists: Mischakoff and Miller)

*13 November 1948
NBC
Studio 8H
Eng/Ger/It AT 125

The soloists came from the front desks of the NBC Orchestra, as was the case with many of Toscanini's performances of concertos and concertante works. There is remarkable integration with the orchestral framework and no question of the two soloists disporting themselves for their own sakes, with occasional interruptions from the orchestra. Even if you are only interested in your favourite violinist or cellist it is worth hearing this for the sake of the work itself, which should be the first consideration.

Serenade no 2 in A, op 16

*27 December 1942
NBC
Studio 8H
Ger/It AT 152

Brahms's two early serenades pay many debts to the eighteenth-century forms of Haydn and Mozart. Toscanini only played odd movements from the First Serenade in his later years, but he broadcast the Second in full with the NBC in 1942. It is scored without violins, and the prevailing viola tone contrasts well with the important wind-writing. The performance is subtly shaped and well recorded.

Haydn Variations (St. Antoni), op 56a

10 April 1936
NY Phil-Sym.
Carnegie Hall
NCRA

4 February 1952
NBC
Carnegie Hall
Eng/Ger/It AT 125

This work was a Toscanini speciality and ought to be included in any representative collection of his recordings. Differences between the Philharmonic-Symphony and the NBC performances are not so marked as with other works he re-recorded. Editions of the NBC version vary from good to excellent. The lightness and refinement of the playing are exemplified in the precision of the woodwind staccato in the vivace six-eight variation. The Philharmonic-Symphony still have the edge, but the NBC replacement is good enough for one not to regret the unavailability of the earlier recording too much. The indispensable early Wagner records are another matter.

Symphony no 1 in C minor, op 68

10 March 1941
NBC
Carnegie Hall
NCRA

6 November 1951
NBC
Carnegie Hall
Eng/Ger/It AT 115

This was the only Brahms symphony that Toscanini officially recorded twice. There are significant differences in the later performance, including a greater expansion that increased clarity and tension. Toscanini included this work in his opening concert with the NBC on Christmas night 1937 and several of the players recalled the excitement of rehearsing with him for the first time. Toscanini drives the music inexorably forward in the first and last movements, sings in the second and brings a pastoral quality to the third. The first-movement climax is shattering and the coda is not laboured with the usual ritardando before the 'meno allegro'. In the finale too the ending is carried through without the traditional holding back of the chorale (though it was here that Toscanini added the controversial timpani-rolls).

Symphony no 2 in D, op 73

11 February 1952
NBC
Carnegie Hall
Eng/Ger/It AT 132

The vividness of the reading still leaves ample room for reflection: no detail, however small, is overlooked. In fact Toscanini's unfolding of the first movement is an object-lesson in proportion, encompassing the symphonic structure with no loss of the music's essential spirit. Nor does the last movement have its back broken with a second subject at half-speed, as sometimes happens: the largamente is again proportionate, and the coda is doubly exciting through being viewed as the logical outcome of the preceding material.

Symphony no 3 in F, op 90

4 November 1952
NBC
Carnegie Hall
Ger/It AT 137

Opinions are divided about this recording. Some have found it sluggish, with brooding tempi and insufficient rhythmic tension; others have admired the weight, breadth and depth of sound (with splendid projection of the brass parts), and have been won over by its singing line. The listener must decide. Unlike the first two symphonies, the first movement is given with the exposition repeat, which in this case is essential to the structure. The German edition is superb.

Symphony no 4 in E minor, op 98

3 December 1951
NBC
Carnegie Hall
Ger/It AT 146

Brahms's craftsmanship and musical stature emerge triumphantly from every bar of this great work, and British listeners old enough to have heard Toscanini conduct it in London in 1935 or 1952 will not forget the overwhelming impression. The first movement in his hands has a searing but classical line and the quasi-scherzo a virile freshness. Most important, the final passacaglia unfolds in a single tempo *as it must*, and even the expressive flute solo in the twelfth variation does not lessen the cumulative effect of the whole. A study of the score is the best antidote to the more 'soulful' interpretations sometimes heard.

CATALANI, Alfredo

Lorelei: Dance of the Water Nymphs (Act 3)
La Wally: Prelude to Act 4

5 August 1952
NBC
Carnegie Hall
Eng/Ger/It AT 109
Ger/It AT 116

A close friendship existed between the composer and the conductor, and Catalani looked on Toscanini as the finest interpreter of his music. One senses this in the passion and commitment of these performances: the extracts are miniatures that illustrate yet another facet of Toscanini's genius.

CHERUBINI, Luigi

(a) Overture: Ali Baba
(b) Ovérture: Anacreon
(c) Overture: Medea

(a) *3 November 1949
NBC
Studio 8H
(b) *21 March 1953
NBC
Carnegie Hall
(c) *18 February 1950
NBC
Studio 8H
Ger/It AT 135

The Maestro helped to explain why Cherubini was so much admired by Beethoven and Berlioz. Only Guido Cantelli seemed likely to follow in his footsteps. *Ali Baba*, in particular, is exceptionally brilliant: note the colourful percussion writing and the feather-lightness of the strings in the coda. The other overtures are played with an almost religious fervour: *Anacreon*, a favoured piece of Toscanini's, is noble, colourful, and exciting in one.

Symphony in D

10 March 1952
NBC
Carnegie Hall
Ger/It AT 135

Those who regard this symphony as a cold and formal work should hear it under Toscanini. The HMV recording is somewhat cloudy, and it comes as a real shock to hear the clarity of the trumpet and drum parts on the German AT.

Requiem Mass in C minor

*18 February 1950
NBC
Studio 8H
Ger/It AT 147

The Requiem might also be considered severe and austere, but what warmth Toscanini extracted from it! Despite the power and intensity of the performance it is the quiet ending that is most moving: a further justification for Beethoven's great admiration of the composer.

141

CIMAROSA, Domenico

Overture: Il Matrimonio per Raggiro

12 November 1949
NBC
Studio 8H
Ger/It AT 134

The performance of this overture is full of brio, but rather on the fierce side. Here the sense of commitment is almost excessive, and the recorded sound does not always flatter.

Overture: Il Matrimonio Segreto

*14 November 1943
NBC
Studio 8H
Ger/It AT 116

Much the same observations apply to this companion piece despite the fact that the performance is six years earlier.

DEBUSSY, Claude

La Mer

8 and 9 February 1942
Philadelphia Orch.
Phil. Academy
Eng/RL 01900 (5)

1 June 1950
NBC
Studio 8H
Franklin Mint
Eng/Ger/It AT 111
Amer/VIC 1246
Fr/RCA VL 4950

Toscanini was adversely criticised for not playing more contemporary works, but in his day he performed a great deal of 'modern music', leaving his younger colleagues to continue with the good work. Here are two examples of his special feelings for Debussy. He played La Mer in Italy in 1909, four years after its first performance. His interpretation is justly famous. He wrote to Debussy suggesting certain adjustments in scoring, such as the doubling of the cellos with violas halfway through the first movement, and had the composer's approval. In fact every detail sounds without fuss, and the sweep and authority are irresistible.

Iberia

18 November 1941
Philadelphia Orch.
Phil. Academy
Eng/RL 0 1900 (5)

2 June 1950
NBC
Studio 8H
Eng/Ger/It AT 111
Amer/VIC 1246
Fr/RCA VL 4950

Iberia, which Toscanini first played in 1918, is not given the most sensuous performance on disc but is second to none for clarity and shading. His approach certainly takes one back to the work again and again for refreshment – and intellectual pleasure.
The Philadelphia records come from the famous sessions in the early 1940s, when Toscanini presumably revelled in the lustrous sounds of the orchestra trained by Stokowski. In general the two performances are similar though they differ in minor details. Such details emerge in both cases with telling clarity, a contrast from the impressionistic vagueness favoured by so many conductors.

DONIZETTI, Gaetano

Overture: Don Pasquale

29 and 30 March 1921
La Scala Orch.
Camden NJ
NCRA

Played like this the overture makes a brilliant concert piece. The inflections and nuances of the cello solo near the beginning are an object-lesson in operatic phrasing. Although the two performances were thirty years apart

5 October 1951
NBC
Carnegie Hall
Ger/It AT 134

the style was so instinctive to Toscanini that differences are minimal. The acoustic recording (La Scala) is a few seconds faster.

DUKAS, Paul

L'Apprenti Sorcier

18 March 1929
NY Phil-Sym.
Carnegie Hall
NCRA

19 March 1950
NBC
Studio 8H
Ger/It AT 142
Amer/RCA VIC 1267
Fr/RCA VL 4950

Associations with Walt Disney's 'Fantasia' have made it difficult for some listeners to hear this piece with an open mind. In spite of the vogue for more heavily characterised performances Toscanini noted that Dukas had called the work a Scherzo and played it accordingly. Those seeking more exaggerated humour should look elsewhere. The 1929 Philharmonic-Symphony record is again famous for its drive and controlled fire, and considering the brevity of the work it is surprising to note that the NBC performance is slower by almost two minutes.

DVORAK, Antonin

Symphony no 9 in E minor (From the New World)

2 February 1953
NBC
Carnegie Hall
Eng/Ger/It AT 114
Amer/RCA VIC 1249
Franklin Mint

As with Beethoven's Fifth many conductors have felt the need to 'interpret' this ever-popular work with frequent tempo-changes, especially in the second subjects of both first and last movements. On the contrary Toscanini performs it with directness and dignity, and and the NBC play as though their lives depended on it. Mention must be made of a magnificent edition of this performance from the Franklin Mint Record Society in 'The 100 Greatest Recordings of all time'. Unfortunately all the current versions suffer from tape deterioration: the American VIC 1249 is the best available.

ELGAR, Sir Edward

Enigma Variations

10 December 1951
NBC
Carnegie Hall
NCRA

When Toscanini played the *Enigma* in London on his famous tour with the New York Philharmonic-Symphony in 1930 many critics found his reading 'un-English' (whatever that may mean). Sir Landon Ronald, a friend of Elgar's, said on the contrary that he considered it one of the greatest he had ever heard and most later commentators have seconded this. The recording preserves a beautifully prepared statement of the score enhanced by superb solo playing and, as always with Toscanini, individual details present themselves with absolute naturalness. This marvellous record was tragically and inexplicably omitted from the RCA re-issue AT series.

FRANCK, César

Symphonic Poem 'Psyché': Psyché and Eros

7 January 1952
NBC
Carnegie Hall
Ger/It AT 142
Fr/RCA VL 4950
Amer/RCA VIC 1246

This seldom-heard extract from Franck's *Psyché* is given an impassioned reading that once again underlines Toscanini's ability to capture the style and spirit of almost any work he prepared. Another Franck tone-poem he played more often was *Les Eolides*: it would have been valuable to have had a commercial recording of that too, as well as of the Symphony in D minor.

GERSHWIN, George

An American in Paris

18 May 1945
NBC
Studio 8H
Eng/Ger/It AT 129

Toscanini showed his obvious respect for Gershwin by playing this as though it were a tone-poem – the jazz style is noticeably absent – and it remains a unique reading of one of the few American works he performed.

GLINKA, Mikhail

Kamarinskaya

*21 December 1940
NBC
Studio 8H
Ger/It VIC 124
Amer/RCA VIC 1245

This effective reading of an attractive and very Russian piece affirms the Maestro's ability to transcend national musical barriers.

GLUCK, Christoph Willibald

(a) Overture, Iphigenia in Aulis
(b) Orfeo: Dance of the Blessed Spirits
(c) Orfeo: Act 2, complete

(a) *22 November 1952
NBC
Carnegie Hall
NCRA
(b) 5 April and
21 November 1929
NY Phil-Sym.
Carnegie Hall
NCRA
4 November 1946
Studio 3A
NCRA
(c) *22 November 1952
NBC
Carnegie Hall
Eng/Ger/It AT 127

Hearing Toscanini's nobly inspired reading of the Overture, which he often included in his American programmes, prompts the question 'why don't we hear more of Gluck?' Many English listeners first became aware of the beauties of *Orfeo* through Kathleen Ferrier's well-loved recording of 'What is Life?' (*Che farò*). The complete second act is a reminder that Toscanini revived the opera at La Scala in 1907 and again at the Met two years later. From the fantastically played Dance of the Furies to Orfeo's entreaties and the serenity of the Dance of the Blessed Spirits (which Toscanini recorded more than once as a separate piece) this is a dramatic but loving performance. Nan Merriman, Barbara Gibson and the Robert Shaw Chorale perform their tasks with comparable devotion.

GROFÉ, Ferde

The Grand Canyon Suite

11 September 1945
NBC
Carnegie Hall
Eng/Ger/It AT 129

Having given the American radio première of Roy Harris's Third Symphony, why did Toscanini play this score? Yet whatever reservations one may have about the musical worth of Grofé's suite it is clear that the NBC Symphony surpassed itself in sheer virtuosity. The trumpet-playing in 'On the Trail' is particularly fine – and if the late John Wayne had turned conductor he could hardly have matched Toscanini's 'Sunset'.

HAYDN, Joseph

Symphony no 88 in G

8 March 1938
NBC
Studio 8H
Ger/It AT 130

The first NBC session, from which this performance dates, must have been memorable if unnerving, bearing in mind Toscanini's long-standing dislike of recording at that time. Playing it to a friend without mentioning the conductor's name, he observed that nobody today plays Haydn with such direct rustic charm and energy.

Symphony no 94 in G ('Surprise')

26 January 1953
NBC
Carnegie Hall
Eng/Ger/It AT 120
Amer/RCA VIC 1262

At the end of a listening session which included four editions of this recording the third movement still seemed too fast, although Haydn marked it 'Allegro molto' and pointed the way to the Beethoven scherzo (e.g. the Fourth Symphony). The rest is beautifully played and the whole well recorded, bringing to life the real humour of the last few bars of the finale.

Symphony no 98 in B flat

25 May 1945
NBC
Studio 8H
NCRA

The JAP is the only LP transfer of Toscanini's recording of this great symphony: as with a few others the purchase is justified in spite of some inevitable duplication.

Symphony no 99 in E flat

*12 March 1949
NBC
Studio 8H
Ger/It AT 149

Toscanini included this several times in his NBC programmes, and played it with polish, warmth and humour, stressing the fresh and robust qualities of the music.

Symphony no 101 in D ('Clock')

29 and 30 March 1929
NY Phil-Sym.
Carnegie Hall
Ger/It AT 130

9 October,
6 November 1946,
and 12 June 1947

The two readings show a noticeable change of style, the easy lyricism and poise of 1929 being replaced by a tighter and more intense vigour. The slow movement is a clear example: the earlier one has a gently flowing melodic line, with subtle tempo inflections to keep it moving; the NBC is more traditionally based and slightly quicker. There is good sound on AT 130 and AT 120.

NBC
Studio 3A
Eng/Ger/It AT 120
Amer/RCA VIC 1262

Sinfonie Concertante in B flat

*6 March 1948
NBC
Studio 8H
Ger/It AT 149

This serenely beautiful performance of one of Haydn's works, with players from the NBC as soloists, came from the same concert as Toscanini's intense and intensely controversial interpretation of the Mozart E flat Symphony (no 39). The sound is excellent.

HÉROLD, Louis

Overture, Zampa

5 August 1952
NBC
Carnegie Hall
Ger/It AT 124

It is said that one sure sign of the great interpreter is the care given to light or lesser music such as this. Certainly no pier orchestra or brass band ever sounded like this: the brass in particular play as one man, and the Maestro gives everything to the task on hand. All editions are excellent.

HUMPERDINCK, Engelbert

Overture, Hansel and Gretel

5 August 1952
NBC
Carnegie Hall
NCRA

Toscanini conducted the opera at La Scala in 1902. This recording of the overture appears to have been over-looked and is not even included in the German AT series, yet it is a perfect example of the NBC's achievement under Toscanini. If all scores of the work disappeared mysteriously overnight it would be practically possible to reconstruct one from the phenomenal transparency of this performance, which moreover adds to the character, even the childlike humour, of the music.

KABALEVSKY, Dmitri

Overture, Colas Breugnon

8 April 1946
NBC
Carnegie Hall
Ger AT 124

Did Toscanini play certain pieces to show off the virtuosity of the NBC Symphony — or was it a desire to introduce new music that had its harmonic roots in the 19th century? The sound is good and clear on AT 124.

KODÁLY, Zoltan

Suite: Háry János

*29 November 1947
NBC
Studio 8H
Eng/Ger/It AT 122

This item in Toscanini's repertory is not so un-expected when we consider his attachment to other works of Kodály, including the *Psalmus Hungaricus* which he performed in Vienna and Budapest with the Vienna Philharmonic in 1934. The humour inherent in

146

the score – the opening 'sneeze' and Napoleon's Army – is subtly drawn and the song element beautifully realised. The rather dry recording does not help the sensuous elements in the music but the reading provides more lasting rewards than those that exaggerate colour and emotion.

LIADOV, Anatol

Kikimora, op 40

29 July 1952
NBC
Carnegie Hall
Ger/It AT 124
Amer/RCA VIC 1245

It is worth following this at least once with the score, noting the orchestral balance and stylistic understanding: yet another example of tension being suitably created in spite of the restrained dynamics of most of the music.

MASSENET, Jules

Scènes Pittoresques: Fête Bohème

3 March 1921
La Scala Orch.
Camden NJ
NCRA

The broadcast of 18 July 1943 included the complete 'Scènes', the only performance of the entire work given by Toscanini during his years in America. The sound of the 1921 recording of this extract is clear enough to give a good indication of the fine quality of the playing.

MENDELSSOHN-BARTHOLDY, Felix

A Midsummer Night's Dream

Scherzo
9 March 1921
La Scala Orch.
Camden NJ
NCRA

30 March 1929
NY Phil-Sym.
Carnegie Hall
NCRA

6 November 1946
NBC
Studio 3A
NCRA

Nocturne and Scherzo
January or
February 1926
NY Phil-Sym.
Carnegie Hall
NCRA

Toscanini's love of Mendelssohn's music is reflected in the many recordings he made of the *Midsummer Night's Dream* Scherzo. As with Beethoven, the conductor pursued his labour beyond the symphonic world into that of chamber music – the Octet and the Quintet op 87 are two familiar examples. He always revealed a blend of mercurial lightness and muscular strength, dispelling the touches of sentimentality that can fault so many Mendelssohn performances. The Philadelphia recording of the more substantial extracts, including the Overture, is recommended on artistic grounds, and the NBC version for good recorded sound. But the famous, nerve-tingling 1929 record of the Scherzo, by the New York Philharmonic-Symphony Orchestra, should certainly not be forgotten.

Incidental Music
11 and 12 January 1942
Philadelphia Orch.
Phil. Academy
Eng/RL 01900 (5)

4 November 1947
NBC
Carnegie Hall
Ger/It AT 138

MENDELSSOHN (cont.)
Octet, op 20

*30 March 1947
NBC
Studio 8H
NCRA

Impressions of a devoted but over-intense reading are liable to change radically with the JAP AT edition which adds depth, warmth and clarity to the strings. This is a performance that no one should judge before hearing AT 1027.

(Scherzo only)
1 June 1945
NBC
Studio 8H
NCRA

Symphony no 4 in A (Italian)

*28 February 1954
NBC
Carnegie Hall
Eng/Ger/It AT 101

This radiant performance highlights many orchestral details lost in many modern stereo records, and the quietness of the studio audience is itself an eloquent tribute to the occasion. Robert C Marsh took Toscanini to task for not including the first-movement repeat with its interesting lead-back, but it is fair to add that the timing of the programme had some bearing on this. Those keen on such details might note that the repeat was observed in a much earlier and lengthier broadcast on 5 February 1938.

Symphony no 5 in D minor (Reformation)

*13 December 1953
NBC
Carnegie Hall
Eng/Ger/It AT 123

Listeners in Britain during the last war may recall the extraordinary impact of a Toscanini-NBC recording of this work relayed by the BBC. The elements of the symphony include Mendelssohn's quotation of *Ein' feste Burg* and the Dresden Amen (more famously used in Wagner's *Parsifal*). The lightness of the scherzo, the unsentimental shaping of the slow movement's cantilena, and the overwhelming climax of the finale with its important timpani part, are matched by worthy recorded quality.

MOZART, Leopold

Toy Symphony

*15 February 1941
NBC

Although long attributed to Haydn, this slight but entertaining piece is now known to have been com-

Studio 8H
Ger/It AT 141

posed by Mozart's father, Leopold. The toys are much in evidence and are, needless to say, played with remarkable precision. (Is it a trifle poker-faced? One would liked to have seen the expression on the faces of the NBC percussion players.)

MOZART, Wolfgang Amadeus

Bassoon Concerto in B flat, K 191
(soloist: Leonard Sharrow)

18 NOvember 1947
NBC
Studio 8H
Ger/It AT 141

A stylishly classical reading with the NBC's first bassoon as soloist. The recording is enjoyable, except perhaps for an over-long first-movement cadenza.

Divertimento in B flat, K 287

Details as above

The recording session obviously went well and the purity of the performance was striking in its day, though the use of multiple strings is questionable, and some may prefer the lighter and more authentic texture of later recordings, such as that by the Vienna Octet. The line, vitality and rhythmic finesse of Toscanini's performance are nonetheless quite remarkable.

Overture: Don Giovanni

*27 January 1946
NBC
Studio 8H
Ger/It AT 134

Toscanini's Mozart problems seem to be epitomised by his last-minute cancellation of the proposed La Scala production in 1929. He plays the Overture for its drama, and although respect for his performance grows with every hearing, many listeners may feel that his approach is too forthright and insufficiently Mozartian.

Overture: The Marriage of Figaro

*8 November 1947
NBC
Studio 8H
Ger/It AT 116

No item was ever thrown away by Toscanini as a mere curtain-raiser. Nevertheless, while this performance may add to one's experience both of *Figaro* and of Mozart, Beecham admirers may well have difficulty in recognising the work.

Overture: The Magic Flute

2 June 1938
BBCSO
Queen's Hall
Ger/DaCa 027 01 0135

*26 November 1949
NBC
Studio 8H
Ger/It AT 134

Those who have heard the private recordings of Toscanini's *Magic Flute* from the 1937 Salzburg Festival will know that the Vienna Philharmonic played this overture like men possessed. The BBC recording was made the following year and is slightly faster than the much later NBC version, which has a fair sound.

Symphony no 35 in D ('Haffner') K385

30 March and
14 April 1929

Much has been written about the differences between these two performances. Toscanini took considerable

NY Phil-Sym.
Carnegie Hall
NCRA

4 November 1946
NBC
Studio 3A
Ger/It AT 126

freedoms in the 1929 recording, which were ironed out in the much stricter and supposedly more classical approach of 1946. Most of the editions issued of the later recording have been flawed by the added reverberation, but the one included in the Victrola VCM box (available only in the UK) is worth acquiring for its clean and natural sound.

Symphony no 39 in E flat, K 543

3rd and 4th movements
17 and 20 December 1946
La Scala Orch.
Camden NJ
NCRA

*6 March 1948
NBC
Studio 8H
Ger/It AT 126

When this recording first appeared in the UK on ALP 1492, the critic Trevor Harvey cautiously remarked that 'no Toscanini performance is without its interest'. The intensity, and the tempo of the minuet, will distress many Mozart-lovers: these features are not so apparent in the 1920 La Scala disc of the third and fourth movements.

Symphony no 40 in G minor, K 550

7 March 1938 and
27 February 1939
NBC
Studio 8H
NCRA

12 March 1950
NBC
Studio 8H
Eng/Ger/It AT 110

For fanatics, Toscanini's reading of this landmark in musical expression is the ultimate. The 1938 performance, one of the earliest of the NBC recordings, retains its interest, but has been supplanted by the preferable sound of the 1950 issue, which is an essential acquisition.

Symphony no 41 in C ('Jupiter') K551

22 June 1945
NBC
Carnegie Hall
Eng/Ger/It AT 110

The finale, with its fusion of sonata form and contrapuntal virtuosity, is one of the miracles of music. Toscanini's performance may be felt to fail gallantly as a result of too fast a tempo, despite the astonishing clarity of the part-writing. The rest is stylistically 'correct', though the old Bruno Walter recording with the Vienna Philharmonic endures in the writer's affection.

MUSSORGSKY, Modest

Pictures at an Exhibition (orch. Ravel)

26 January 1953
NBC
Carnegie Hall
Eng/GerIt AT 107
Amer/RCA VIC 1273

This is an essential Toscanini disc, with splendid sound on both the English and the German AT versions. The brilliance and accuracy of the playing, with one miracle following another, are capped by a 'Great Gate of Kiev' that is shattering in its impact. Again, we experience Toscanini's unique capacity for holding power in reserve for the climax of a work.

PAGANINI, Niccolo

Moto Perpetuo, op 11 (arr. Toscanini)

17 April 1939
NBC
Studio 8H
NCRA

It may have been pride in his orchestral strings that prompted Toscanini to arrange and record this virtuoso piece, in which the solo violin part is played in unison and *en masse*.

PIZZETTI, Ildebrando

La Pisanelle (No. 2: The Port at Famagusta)

20 December 1920
La Scala Orch.
Camden NJ
NCRA

Toscanini championed a great deal of music by lesser Italian composers, and probably regarded Pizzetti as an English conductor might view either Bax or Ireland. The music is sufficiently attractive to make one wish for a recording of the complete work.

PONCHIELLI, Amilcare

La Gioconda: The Dance of the Hours

29 July 1952
NBC
Carnegie Hall
Eng/Ger/It AT 109
Amer/RCA VIC 1263

Even if this had been a great masterpiece it could hardly have been prepared with more loving care, for Toscanini demanded the highest standards whatever the occasion. It comes as a revelation in the playing of 'light music'. The recording itself is excellent, wide-ranging and beautifully balanced by mono standards.

PROKOFIEV, Sergei

Classical Symphony

15 October 1951
NBC
Carnegie Hall
Eng/Ger/It AT 122

Toscanini gave three performances of this popular work in 1929 with the New York Philharmonic-Symphony Orchestra, and six performances – at widely-spaced intervals – with the NBC. It was in fact the only piece by Prokofiev he ever played, and it is easy to understand his affection for its clear-cut form and consciously traditional harmonies. With the passage of time he took a more leisurely view of the slow movement, taking it far more slowly in the 1951 recording than in his earlier performances.

PUCCINI, Giacomo

La Bohème

*3 and 10 February 1946
NBC
Studio 8H
Eng/Ger/It AT 203 (2)
Amer/VIC VICS 6019

It is a matter of musical history that Toscanini gave this opera its world première in 1896 – half-a-century before the broadcast from which this recording was taken. The performance is so vivid and the involvement so complete that it is hard to believe that it all took place in a studio. Greater singing may be heard elsewhere, but the service to Puccini is paramount. The Maestro's spontaneous vocal contributions, turning solos into duets and duets into trios, are more touching than intrusive. The English AT version is adequate, the German remarkably good, but the American Victrola edition is even better.

RAVEL, Maurice

Daphnis and Chloe: 2nd Suite

21 November 1949
NBC
Carnegie Hall
Eng/Ger/It AT 107
Fr/RCA VL 4950
Amer/RCA VIC 1273

The excitement captured in this recording defies description. Everything is utterly disciplined, from the radiant sunrise and the exquisite flute-playing to the dizzy virtuosity of the *Danse Générale*. Each edition has successively revealed more of these glories.

RESPIGHI, Otterino

Roman Festivals

19 November 1941
Philadelphia Orch.
Phil. Academy
Eng/RL 01900 (5)

12 December 1949
NBC
Carnegie Hall
Ger/It AT 142

Toscanini's flair for his compatriot's music is understandable. Indeed, it can be argued that he makes Respighi's trilogy sound better than it actually is. The NBC give a breathtaking performance – full of poetry and excitement.

The Fountains of Rome

17 December 1951
NBC
Carnegie Hall
Eng/Ger/It AT 100
Amer/RCA VIC 124

Contrary to some reports, Toscanini did not present the world première of this work which was, in fact, a disaster. He did, however, 'rescue' it, and if his earlier performances were to the standard of this 1951 version Respighi was fortunate indeed to have such a champion. Great delicacy of writing and powerful climaxes reveal it as probably the most convincing of the three works.

The Pines of Rome

17 March 1953
NBC
Carnegie Hall
*Catalogue numbers
as above*

Toscanini included this work in his first concert with the New York Philharmonic-Symphony Orchestra in 1926: characteristically he repeated the whole programme in its entirety on his very last appearance with the orchestra 19 years later.

Ancient Airs and Dances: Gagliarda

18 December 1920
La Scala Orch.
Camden NJ
NCRA

Respighi's suites of arrangements have become extremely popular in recent years. Toscanini's remarkably early recording of a fragment of the work reveals the more gentle aspect of Respighi's art.

ROSSINI, Gioacchino

Many other conductors have tried to emulate Toscanini's performances of Rossini overtures, but none

152

has achieved so perfect a fusion of wit and brilliance, dignity and eloquence. Of the nine available, four were recorded twice. The later NBC versions, although very fine, do not replace the earlier classic recordings which Toscanini made with the New York Philharmonic-Symphony Orchestra.

Overture: The Barber of Seville

21 November 1929
NY Phil-Sym.
Carnegie Hall
NCRA

This first pair of recordings exemplifies the point made above, and it is a matter of great regret that the 1929 version is not available at the time of going to press: let up hope that RCA will soon rectify the situation.

28 June 1945
NBC
Carnegie Hall
Eng/Ger/It AT 108
Amer/RCA VIC 1274

Overture: La Cenerentola

28 June 1945
NBC
Eng/Ger/It AT 108
Amer/RCA VIC 1248

All the Toscanini hallmarks are captured in this recording of one of the less well-known of Rossini's overtures.

Overture: L'Italiana in Algeri

10 April 1936
NY Phil-Sym.
Carnegie Hall
NCRA

Comments apply here as with the 'Barber'. When one hears so many conductors starting the *crescendi* too early and reaching a peak too soon one appreciates Toscanini's greatness all the more.

*14 April 1950
NBC
Carnegie Hall
Ger/It AT 116
Amer/RCA VIC 1248

Overture: La Scala di Seta

13 June 1938
BBCSO
Queen's Hall
Ger/DaCa 027 01 035

Beecham and Toscanini can be directly compared in their famous recordings of this piece. One Beecham supporter would have us believe that Toscanini's reading produces a ladder of steel, not of silk: on the other hand, many find Beecham's interpretation somewhat over-refined. In the Toscanini recording, the delicacy and unanimity with which the violins launch the main section show how well the BBC players rose to the occasion. There is a surprising and subtle change of pace for the second subject.

Overture: The Siege of Corinth

14 June 1945
NBC

This offers a magisterial reading of one of Rossini's larger-scale overtures, which includes some Beethoven-

Carnegie Hall
Ger/It AT 134
Amer/RCA VIC 1248

10 April 1936
NY Phil-Sym.
Carnegie Hall
NCRA

28 September 1951
NBC
Carnegie Hall
Eng/Ger/It AT 108
Amer/RCA VIC 1274

8 June 1945
NBC
Carnegie Hall
Eng/Ger/It AT 108
Amer/RCA VIC 1274

Details as above

1 March 1939
NY Phil-Sym.
Carnegie Hall
NCRA

19 January 1953
NBC
Studio 8H
Eng/Ger/It AT 108

8 June 1945
NBC
Carnegie Hall
Eng/Ger/It AT 109
Amer/RCA VIC 1274

1 June 1950
NBC
Studio 8H

like gestures and even some fugal writing. The recording
suffers some loss of clarity through excessive reverberation.

Overture: Semiramide
The New York Philharmonic-Symphony version is
incomparable, although the NBC performance does contain some marvellous details. Listen to the string
playing at the start of the *allegro*, the superbly controlled
crescendi, the clarinet solo from bar 183 and the conversational treatment of the strings in bars 233-8.

Overture: Il Signor Bruschino
This is the overture in which the violins tap the music
stands with their bows: the performance has plenty of
charm as well as humour.

Overture: La Gazza Ladra
This piece, with its arresting opening, was the first
music Toscanini conducted on his return to La Scala in
1946. The NBC recording does more than justice to the
grandeur of the introduction, and to the grace and wit of
the rest.

Overture: William Tell
Although 14 years separate these two readings, the
relative timings vary by only eleven seconds: of the two,
the 1953 version is the slower. Outstanding features are
the timpani during the storm, the tasteful rubato in
the pastoral section and the subtle inflections of the
virtuoso string passages in the finale. It is curious that
Toscanini doubles the solo cello parts at the opening.

William Tell: Passo a Sei
One of the many delights is the fractional holding
back of the upbeat into the rondo-theme on its return:
another is the charm of the oboe and clarinet episodes,
and yet another the perfect integration of the busier
accompanying figures in the later stages.

SAINT-SAËNS, Camille

Danse Macabre
This is a well-considered reading of a once-popular
work that seems, like its dancing skeletons, to have died
a natural death in recent years.

Ger/It AT 150
Fr/RCA VL 4950
Amer/RCA VIC 1244

Symphony no 3

*15 November 1952
NBC
Carnegie Hall
Ger/It AT 150
Fr/RCA VL 4950

Toscanini presented this symphony several times in his earlier years, but only once during his time with the NBC. It is fortunate that such an astounding performance was preserved. Whereas many have conducted the symphony for its sensational and superficial effects, Toscanini gave it the kind of care and concentration appropriate to Beethoven's Ninth. The controlled brilliance of the last few pages alone places this among the great Toscanini recordings.

SCHUBERT, Franz

Symphony no 5 in B flat

17 March 1953
NBC
Carnegie Hall
Eng/Ger/It AT 123

Interpretations have differed widely over the *allegro* of the first movement. Bruno Walter and Beecham (in both his commercial recordings) adopted a rather leisurely tempo. On the other hand, Fritz Busch, Erich Kleiber and Toscanini take it at a brisk pace which, apart from anything else, emphasises the difference in mood between the first two movements.

Symphony no 8 in B minor ('Unfinished')

12 March 1950
NBC
Studio 8H
Eng/Ger/It AT 101

The contrast between the two movements of the 'Unfinished' Symphony presents a problem of interpretation. Some conductors make little distinction between them in terms of tempi, and so miss the full drama of the development in the first movement. Toscanini, as one might expect, emphasises the difference. In passing, it should be noted that in a 1939 broadcast he made the exposition repeat, but did not do so in this 1950 recording.

Symphony no 9 in C

16 November 1941
Philadelphia Orch.
Phil. Academy
Eng/Ger/It AT 102
Eng/RL 01900 (5)

25 February 1947
NBC
Carnegie Hall
NCRA

9 February 1953
NBC

The two later readings with the NBC are very similar, though remarks are confined to the 1953 performance as the 1947 version is not available at present except in the JAP 100 edition (AT 1024).

Toscanini's approach to Schubert has been criticised as both ruthless and relentless, but a good deal of such criticism stems from an easy-going tradition which surrounds this great architectural masterpiece in music. The Maestro's absorption with the composer's written indications, and his refusal to undermine the unity of the work with violent changes of tempo in the second subject and in the coda of the first movement, is of the utmost significance. His unfailing sense of balance

Carnegie Hall
Ger/It AT 151

is always at the service of the glorious scoring: to mention just one point – the pianissimo trombones (Tovey's *locus classicus*) can never have been heard to better advantage.

The Philadelphia performance survives as a result of the devotion of the recording engineer John Corbett, who spent no less than 750 hours on the ill-fated original masters, removing clicks and other faults. This reading differs from the later NBC versions in its heavier inflections, and the marvellous Philadelphia sound places it in a category of its own.

SCHUMANN, Robert

Overture: Manfred

11 November 1946
NBC
Carnegie Hall
NCRA

Toscanini was not the only great conductor to adjust Schumann's scoring in order to achieve a better balance. Nothing better exemplifies his ability to express drama and passion within the constraints imposed by a basic tempo. The precise timing of the trumpet entry at the start of the *Allegro* illustrates this point perfectly.

Symphony no 3 (Rhenish)

*12 November 1949
NBC
Studio 8H
Ger/It AT 138

Although this is one of Toscanini's greatest recorded performances every edition is over-modulated. The only way to compensate for this is to use tone controls in order to increase the bass and diminish the treble.

SHOSTAKOVICH, Dmitri

Symphony no 1

*12 March 1944
NBC
Studio 8H
Ger/It AT 205 (2)

As one might expect, Toscanini resisted the temptation to conduct this work at speeds well below those indicated by the composer. As a result, the *Scherzo* may sound too fast to some ears, but the reading remains totally authentic and the recorded sound quality is good throughout.

Symphony no 7 (Leningrad)

*19 July 1942
NBC
Studio 8H
Catalogue nos.
as above

It may have been Toscanini's admiration for the Russian people during the critical years of World War II that persuaded him to present this work, for in later years he he declared that he 'must have been mad' to have learned it. The overall effect is certainly over-blown, and Shostakovich himself is said to have disliked this performance for reasons which were not made clear.

SIBELIUS, Jean

Finlandia

5 August 1952
NBC

This is a perfect example of a familiar war-horse sounding fresh and new under Toscanini's baton,

Carnegie Hall
Eng/Ger/It AT 122
Amer/RCA VIC 1245

with the added advantage of excellent recorded sound throughout.

Pohjola's Daughter

7 December 1940
NBC
Studio 8H
Ger AT 139

It is tragic that Toscanini's incomparable performances of *The Swan of Tuonela, En Saga* and the Fourth Symphony are apparently not available. *Pohjola's Daughter*, which he performed only once in his career, is welcome for its melodic directness. This beautiful work is included in the German edition of the Second Symphony but not in the Italian edition, a fact which the latter sleeve-note fails to make clear.

Symphony no 2 in D

Details as above

Toscanini's approach to this work looks forward to the later symphonies, especially nos 3 and 5, and does not hark back to the rather unrepresentative First Symphony. In this respect, as in many others, he anticipated the modern tradition, and the creative energy which he unleashes in this performance is spine-tingling.

SMETANA, Bedrich

Ma Vlast: Vltava (Moldau)

19 March 1950
NBC
Studio 8H
Eng/Ger AT 124
Amer/RCA VIC 1245

This completely Italian reading is enjoyable because it is so perfectly shaped and deeply felt. However this may not suit all tastes: those who seek the strongly nationalistic elements in this work may criticise Toscanini's interpretation as unidiomatic.

SMITH, John Stafford

The Star-Spangled Banner (arr. Toscanini)

19 March 1942
NBC
Carnegie Hall
NCRA

Although Toscanini adamantly refused to play the Fascist *Giovinezza* he performed many other national anthems, as the occasion demanded, with dignity and fervour. This version was a memorable feature of many of his NBC concerts.

SOUSA, John Philip

El Capitan/Stars and Stripes Forever

18 May 1945
NBC
Studio 8H
NCRA

The energy and panache with which Toscanini despatched these pieces is unlikely to be equalled. The spontaneity and clarity of the famous combination of themes at the end of *Stars and Stripes Forever* have to be heard to be believed.

STRAUSS, Johann

The Blue Danube

11 December 1941
and 10 March 1942

There are plenty of 'idiomatic' recordings of this most famous of all Viennese waltzes, but Toscanini's is not

157

NBC
Carnegie Hall
Ger/It AT 118

one of them. Robert C Marsh spoke of 'the bloodless, mechanical execution of the figures': be that as it may, there remain details, including the shaping of the introduction, that have their own distinctive beauty.

Tritsch-Tratsch Polka (arr. Toscanini)

6 May 1941
NBC
Carnegie Hall
*Catalogue nos
as above*

This is entertaining and well-recorded for its time.

STRAUSS, Richard

Don Juan

10 January 1951
NBC
Carnegie Hall
Carnegie Hall
Eng/Ger/It AT 105
Amer/RCA VIC 1267

This is outstanding even among Toscanini performances. Its incandescent quality is impossible to describe in words, and the fullest orchestral sonorities are so marvellously balanced that important inner voices, normally lost, are heard with absolute clarity.

Tod und Verklärung

8 January 1942
Philadelphia Otch.
Phil. Academy
Eng/RL 01900 (5)

10 March 1952
NBC
Carnegie Hall
Eng/Ger/It AT 105

Despite the petty rivalry between Strauss and Toscanini over the première of *Salome*, the Maestro remained one of the most eloquent champions of the early tone poems. He played *Tod und Verklärung* more than any other during his time in New York, and invested the more banal passages with a sublime dignity. The opening always gave him trouble, as an unofficial recording of a rehearsal confirms, but there is no hint of this on either of the published versions.

Till Eulenspiegel

4 November 1952
NBC
Carnegie Hall
Eng/Ger/It AT 105

This performance is unconventional to a fascinating degree, many of the tempi being surprisingly slow. Toscanini played the work in Italy as early as 1902 with great success. In his hands, the episodes are totally integrated with the recurrent 'rondo' idea, and the final trial scene has a superhuman weight and sound quality which, if contemporary accounts are to be believed, fulfilled the intentions of the composer's own performances..

Don Quixote
(soloists: Frank Miller and Carlton Cooley)

*22 November 1953
NBC
Carnegie Hall
Ger/It AT 148

The German edition of this is one of the finest and most natural-sounding of all available Toscanini recordings. He made an unforgettable impression in London with this work which he conducted in 1938 with Feuermann as cellist. The recorded performance is all the more remarkable when it is remembered that it was taken from an unedited broadcast during the conductor's last season with the NBC.

SUPPÉ, Franz von

Overture: Poet and Peasant

*18 July 1943
NBC
Studio 8H
Ger/It AT 124

During the NBC wartime years Toscanini included in his concerts several well-worn favourites such as this, but always managed to present them in a new and vivid light.

TCHAIKOVSKY, Peter Ilyich

Piano Concerto no 1 in B flat minor
(soloist: Vladimir Horowitz)

6 and 14 May 1941
NBC
Carnegie Hall
Eng AT 113
Amer/RCA VIC 1554

*25 April 1943
NBC
Carnegie Hall
Ger/It AT 113
Amer/RCA LM 2319
Eng/RCA VH 015

The first of these two performances was recorded in 1941 and its sound was notoriously poor, even by the standards of the day. The second comes from a Tchaikovsky concert given on 25 April 1943 (which, incidentally, raised 11 million dollars for War Bonds) and has all the added excitement of a public performance. Keen collectors will undoubtedly want both editions, but LM 2319 is by far the best-sounding version, and is currently available in Britain from import dealers.

Symphony no 6 (Pathétique)

8 February 1942
Phildelphia Orch.
Phil. Adademy
Eng/RL 01900 (5)

24 November 1947
NBC
Carnegie Hall
Ger/Eng/It AT 104
Amer/RCA VIC 1268

It is an extraordinary fact that Toscanini first conducted Tschaikovsky's last symphony just four years after its composition – in Turin in 1897. His approach may be described as a much-needed corrective in which the symphonic structure emerges with great force and dignity. The scherzo-cum-march is, needless to say, carried through with great effect, and the alternating grace and pathos of the preceding five-four movement are perfectly realised. Much salvage work had to be done on the 1942 Philadelphia recording: the results are not quite up to the standards set by the Schubert Ninth Symphony edition, but more than enough remains to reveal the superlative quality of the playing.

Manfred Symphony

5 December 1949
NBC
Carnegie Hall
Ger/It AT 145
Amer/RCA VICS 1315

Toscanini seemed to regard this neglected work as 'an opera without voices' but, as in the opera house, his fiery discipline yielded human warmth as well. He made some adjustments to the scoring, adding horns at the opening, and overcame his usual scruples by making a substantial cut in the last movement. Unfortunately, tape splices can be clearly heard both in the first movement and in the finale, and

159

the situation is further complicated by the fact that various deleted editions actually contain different splices!

Nutcracker Suite

19 November 1951
NBC
Carnegie Hall
Eng/Ger/It AT 118
Amer/RCA VIC 1263

This Suite appeared in the very first symphony concert conducted by Toscanini, on 20 March 1896. More than half-a-century later he was still conducting it with a finesse the work rarely receives.

('Waltz of the Flowers'
only)
Eng/Ger/It AT 119

Fantasy Overture: Romeo and Juliet

8 April 1946
NBC
Carnegie Hall
Eng/Ger/It AT 119
Amer/RCA VIC 1245

The NBC session in April 1946 during which this work was recorded also yielded extracts from Berlioz's *Romeo and Juliet*: taken together they present an interesting comparison of style and treatment. The Tchaikovsky score is imbued with a passion that is never torn to shreds, although Toscanini does allow a few extra cymbal clashes in the brawl scenes. The love music is tender, but without sentimentality, and there is an overwhelming climax in the return of the famous theme.

THOMAS, Ambroise

Overture: Mignon

19 March 1942
NBC
Carnegie Hall
NCRA

It is ironic that this lightweight piece – enjoyable and brilliantly played as it is – is recorded to standards rarely achieved in Toscanini's records of more serious and important works.

29 July 1952
NBC
Carnegie Hall
Ger/It AT 116

VERDI, Giuseppe

Aida

Complete:
*26 March and
2 April 1949
NBC
Studio 8H
Eng/Ger/It AT 302 (3)
Amer/RCA VICS 6113 (3)

Preludes only:
Ger/It AT 304 (3)

A recording of Toscanini rehearsing parts of *Aida* has been released in Italy. Either by fate or coincidence his professional conducting career started and finished with this opera. In 1886 he made his legendary début with the work in Rio de Janeiro at a moment's notice, and his very last assignment (in June 1954) was the remaking of parts of the recorded 1949 broadcast.
What makes this set so valuable is not the individual singing, some of which is indifferent, but the uniquely thrilling conception of the whole work, and the justice

Ballet music only:
Eng/Ger/It AT 109

done to the spirit of Verdi. The German edition is recommended.

Un Ballo in Maschera

Complete:
*17 and 24 January 1954
NBC
Carnegie Hall
Eng/Ger/It AT 300

This is the best sounding of all Toscanini's recordings of complete operas, and probably contains the finest singing as well. It is hard to believe that it took place before an audience in Carnegie Hall only a few weeks before Toscanini's final and tragic Wagner concert. Two points will serve to illustrate the range of his undimmed art: the shattering climax as Amelia draws the name of the assassin, and the exquisite elegance and poise of the stage-band's mazurka in the final scene.

Preludes only:
Ger/It AT 304 (3)

Falstaff

*1 and 8 April 1950
NBC
Studio 8H
Eng/Ger/It AT 301 (3)
Amer/RCA LM 6111 (3)

This was one of Toscanini's incomparable achievements. Memories still abound of his Salzburg performances in the 1930s, and a recording of poor quality exists of one of them. The NBC Orchestra of the 1950s did not have quite the refinement of the Vienna Philharmonic Orchestra, and neither was Valdengo to be compared with Mariano Stabile. Nevertheless, the verve, the humanity, the ensemble work and the sheer musicality of every bar make this one of the most treasured items in the legacy. The sound is good in all editions.

Overture: La Forza del Destino

28 June 1945
Carnegie Hall
NCR

10 November 1952
NBC
Carnegie Hall
Ger/It AT 304 (3)
Amer/RCA VIC 1248

The two performances are similar in their incandescence and beauty of line, although the 1952 version is obviously preferable in terms of sound. An interesting sidelight: in some editions of the later performance Toscanini can be heard saying 'Si, caro' in the silent pause at bar 123 (presumably an encouragement to the clarinet). However, the intervention is not audible on an HMV/ALP pressing auditioned.

I Lombardi: 'Qui posa il fianco'

Details as above

At one of the rehearsals for this Trio from Act 3 of *I Lombardi* Toscanini arrived late – a rare occurrence – trailing behind Mischa Mischakoff, leader of the NBC. The reason soon became obvious: a separate rehearsing of the concerto-like violin solo that opens the scene. The singers rise to the occasion, although the quality of the recorded sound is not flattering.

Luisa Miller: Overture and Aria 'Quando le sere'

*25 July 1943
NBC
Studio 8H

These extracts opened the historic all-Verdi concert on 25 July 1943 during the course of which Mussolini's downfall was announced. Toscanini was an implacable

161

Catalogue nos as above

enemy of the dictator, and it was appropriate in the extreme that together with his hero Verdi he should have had the last word over Fascism in Italy.

Nabucco: 'Va pensiero'

*31 January 1943
NBC
Studio 8H
Catalogue nos as above

The recording conveys the quality of this deeply-felt reading, although the performance given at the re-opening of La Scala in 1946 was, by all accounts, even more moving.

Otello

Complete:
*6 and 13 December 1947
NBC
Studio 8H
Ger/It AT 303 (3)

Preludes, Act IV only:
Recording details as above
Ger/It AT 304 (3)

Ballet Music only:
*13 March 1948
NBC
Studio 8H
Eng/Ger/It AT 109

If one had only six minutes to exemplify Toscanini's genius, the opening scene of this opera would make an excellent choice. His intimate knowledge of the work dated from the very first performance in 1887, when he played second cello. In fact, he was criticised by Verdi for following the dynamic markings too closely: the composer felt that his playing in the famous passage at the end of Act 1 was too quiet. The 1947 NBC broadcast was a revelation even for those who considered they knew the opera well. Of the available editions, the German one is recommended.

Rigoletto: Act 4

25 May 1944
NBC
Madison Square Gardens
Ger/It AT 304

Although Toscanini occasionally conducted operatic extracts in his concerts, this performance of a complete act was the most significant event for opera-lovers since his departure from the Metropolitan in 1915. The occasion was a charity concert at Madison Square which featured the combined forces of the NBC and the New York Philharmonic-Symphony orchestras. Among the excellent cast, Milanov is outstanding as Gilda.

La Traviata

Complete:
*1 and 8 December 1946
NBC
Studio 8H
Eng/Ger/It AT 202 (2)
Amer/RCA LM 6002(2)

Preludes, Act I and III
18 March 1929
NY Phil-Sym.
Carnegie Hall
NCRA

*10 March 1941
NBC Carnegie Hall

This much-debated recording was justifiably criticised for its poor sound quality, but complaints that Toscanini's direction is too tense are another matter. Spike Hughes maintained that Toscanini presented the work not as a singers' opera, nor even as a conductor's opera but as a composer's opera. The evidence of the score is there to confirm this view, although many of Toscanini's tempi are, in fact slower than Verdi's metronome markings. Riccardo Muti has described Toscanini's pianissimi as having the power to 'cut like a knife', and the recording of the Preludes clearly exemplifies this. As for recorded quality, the English edition is fair, the German and Italian are better, and the American LM version recommended.

162

Eng/Ger5It AT 304 (3)
Amer/RCA VIC 1248

Overture: I Vespri Siciliani

*24 January 1942
NBC
Studio 8H
Ger/It AT 116/304 (3)
Amer/RCA VIC 1248

This recording shows what can happen when such a work is given the dedication appropriate to a Beethoven symphony. Toscanini's belief in the greatness of even the lesser-known Verdi is helped by the recorded quality.

Hymn of the Nations

8 and 10 December 1943
NBC
Studio 8H
Ger/It AT 304 (3)

This occasional piece was composed for the International Exhibition in London, held in 1862. When it was featured as a climax in a wartime film made with the NBC, Toscanini added both the 'Internationale' and 'The Star-Spangled Banner' to Verdi's parade of national anthems. The original recording was very dry but has since been improved: nevertheless it still needs careful control.

Four Sacred Pieces: Te Deum

*14 March 1954
NBC
Carnegie Hall
Eng/Ger/It AT 132

Many of those who heard Toscanini conduct this work in live performances still vividly recall the extraordinary impact of the first full choral entry. The effect is slightly lost on the English pressing, but is there in full measure on the German edition.

Toscanini often performed this beautiful, meditative piece as a prelude to the *Requiem*. He included it in the memorable NBC programme on 14 March 1954, which also contained the Prologue to Boito's *Mefistofele*.

Requiem

*27 January 1951
NBC
Carnegie Hall
Eng/Ger/It AT 201 (2)
Amer/RCA LM 6108 (2)

Many critics have claimed that this recording is absolutely indispensable to all those who love the work. Toscanini first conducted the *Requiem* in Milan in 1902, when the audience gave him a standing ovation after the 'Dies Irae'. His reading of the work has long been a *locus classicus*, although this 1951 recording is tighter and less spacious than, for example, the pre-war performances he gave in Salzburg and in London. Robert C Marsh wrote of the recording that 'the soloists (sometimes) appear trapped in the unyielding framework of Toscanini's concept of the score', but the splendour of that concept and the marvel of its result are beyond all doubt. The English edition shows a marked tape-deterioration: the German issue is much to be preferred.

WAGNER, Richard

A Faust Overture

11 November 1946
NBC

This early but forward-looking work of Wagner created an extraordinary impression when Toscanini included it

163

Carnegie Hall
Ger/It AT 400 (4)
Amer/RCA VIC 1247

in his 1935 programmes with the BBC in London, and the 1946 recorded NBC performance is far less expansive in the second-subject material. An academic point: Toscanini played E natural in the *ff* statement of the main theme in the earlier performances but 'corrected' it to E flat later. The NBC recording is adequate.

Die Götterdämmerung: Siegfried's Rhine Journey

8 February and
9 April 1936
NY Phil-Sym.
Carnegie Hall
NCRA

17 March 1941
NBC
Carnegie Hall
NCRA

The 1936 performance is more spacious than its successors, and the precision and sonority are breathtaking. The earlier of the two NBC readings is available only in the JAP 100 edition. The later recording (1949), though thrilling enough, has been criticised for its quicker tempo. The fabricated ending is an unavoidable embarrassment.

22 December 1949
NBC
Carnegie Hall
Ger/It AT 400 (4)

Die Götterdämmerung: Funeral Music

24 February 1941
NBC
Carnegie Hall
NCRA

3 January 1952
NBC
Carnegie Hall
Ger/It AT 400 (4)
Amer/RCA VICS 1316

The French composer and conductor Inghelbrecht gave an impressive account of Toscanini rehearsing this extract, and the way in which he insisted on an accurate and unhurried treatment of the important triplet-figure in the basses. 'I have given this triplet lesson in vain all over the world', he said. The grandeur and nobility of the reading are enhanced by many such details: those who prefer a weightier and more Germanic interpretation can always turn to Furtwängler.

Die Götterdämmerung:
Daybreak and Siegfried-Brünnhilde Duet
(soloists: Traubel and Melchior)

*22 February 1941
NBC
Carnegie Hall
Ger/It AT 400 (4)
Amer/RCA VIC 1369

After so many extracts adapted for orchestra it is good to have this scene intact, with two such splendid singers. Toscanini first conducted the opera at Turin in 1895. The recording derives from a Wagner concert given with the NBC.

Die Götterdämmerung: Brünnhilde's Immolation
(soloist: Helen Traubel)

24 February 1941
all other details as above

This comes from another Wagner programme given only two days after the one containing the Traubel-Melchior duet. From all points of view it is one of Toscanini's greatest Wagner recordings, ineffably tender in the section beginning 'Wie Sonne lauter strahlt mir sein Licht', and shattering in the intensity and control of the final cataclysm. Can the Maestro be heard singing the missing Hagen's 'Zurück vom Ring!' in the midst of the general turmoil?

Lohengrin: Prelude to Act 1

8 February and
9 April 1936
NT Phil-Sym.
Carnegie Hall
NCRA

24 February and
6 May 1941
NBC
Carnegie Hall
NCRA

22 October 1951
NBC
Carnegie Hall
Ger/It AT 400 (4)
Amer/RCA VIC 1247

Toscanini's love of Wagner's music dated from 1884 when, as a cello student, he took part in a performance of *Lohengrin* given at Parma.
The early New York Philharmonic-Symphony recordings may be preferred for its greater warmth, but the far greater presence of the 1951 recording weighs heavily in the balance.

Lohengrin: Prelude to Act 3

1936 and 1951
entries as above

The attack at the outset and the complete integration of the middle section elevate this war-horse into far more than an 'effective' concert-piece.

Die Meistersinger: Preludes to Act 1 and 3

11 March 1946 (Act I)
26 November 1951 (Act III)
NBC
Carnegie Hall
Ger/It AT 400 (4)
Amer/RCA VIC 1247

'It is like a dream', Toscanini remarked when he heard a private recording of one of his Salzburg performances of *Die Meistersinger*. His devotion to this masterpiece, with which he launched his first La Scala season in 1898, is reflected in the noble, transparent reading of the Overture, and the profound humanity of the Act 3 Prelude, in which the timing of the brass entries is so perfectly realised.

Parsifal: Prelude to Act I and Good Friday Spell

22 December 1949
NBC
Carnegie Hall
Ger/It AT 400 (4)
Amer/RCA VIC 1278

It may surprise Toscanini's later listeners to learn that his *Parsifal* at Bayreuth in 1931 was by far the slowest performance ever given there. The extracts on this record are most beautifully played, and the rapt mood of the Good Friday music is well conveyed in the recording. The sudden *pp* in the strings just before the B major oboe theme begins is one of so many miraculous details.

Tristan and Isolde: Prelude and Liebestod

7 January 1952
NBC
Carnegie Hall

We can only lament the lack of a complete recording of *Tristan* which Toscanini produced early on in Turin and Milan and with which he created such a sensation

Ger/It AT 400 (4)
Amer/RCA VIC 1278

Liebestod only:
19 March 1942
NBC
Carnegie Hall
NCRA

at Bayreuth in 1930. His reading of the Prelude with its revelations of internal balance and climax is offset by his attention to the Liebestod, so ineffectual without Isolde, though the recording is beautiful throughout.

Die Walküre: Act 1, Scene 3
(soloists: Traubel and Melchior)

*22 February 1941
NBC
Carnegie Hall
Ger/It AT 400 (4)
Amer/RCA VICS 1316

Memories of the Lehmann-Melchior recording with Bruno Walter do not efface the value of this issue, which harks back to Toscanini's conception of the work during his early days at La Scala. A rehearsal record of this performance has been published in Italy on CLS/HDEL 12807.

Die Walküre: Ride of the Valkyries

11 March 1946
NBC
Carnegie Hall
NCRA

This monstrous so-called extract, which may have had some point in the days before radio and records made the music more accessible in its proper context, is played with great energy and is acceptably recorded.

3 January 1952
NBC
Carnegie Hall
Ger/It AT 400 (4)
Amer/RCA VICS 1316

Siegfried: Forest Murmurs

29 October 1951
NBC
Carnegie Hall
Catalogue nos as above

The same remarks apply here, but although the wood-bird remains obstinately inarticulate the playing is at least a reminder of Toscanini's incomparable services to Wagner in the theatre.

Siegfried Idyll

6 February and
9 April 1936
NY Phil-Sym.
Carnegie Hall
NCRA

These performances vary in subtle detail, but the old Philharmonic-Symphony version and the second NBC recording are similar in their simple dignity and natural flow. The 1946 version is warmer in sound, and slightly faster.

11 March 1946
NBC
Carnegie Hall
NCRA

29 July 1952
NBC Carnegie Hall
Ger/It AT 400 (4)
Amer/RCA VIC 1247

WALDTEUFEL, Emile

The Skaters' Waltz

28 June 1945
NBC
Carnegie Hall
Ger/It AT 118

Robert C Marsh summed up this record as 'a pleasant old-fashioned waltz turned into a stunning concert piece'. It dates from an NBC recording session in June 1945 thereby missing the 'live concert' atmosphere that enhances Toscanini's playing of other popular favourites.

WEBER, Carl Maria von

Invitation to the Dance (arr. Berlioz)

14 June 1938
BBCSO
Queen's Hall
Ger/DaCa 027 01 0135

28 September 1951
NBC
Carnegie Hall
Ger/It AT 118

Toscanini included this piece in the first of his London programmes in 1938 and recorded it with the BBC Symphony Orchestra shortly afterwards. The panache of Berlioz's scoring and, indeed, Toscanini's conducting, is clearly conveyed in both recordings.

Overture: Euryanthe

29 October 1951
NBC
Carnegie Hall
Ger/It AT 134

Euryanthe was given its long-delayed Italian première by Toscanini at La Scala, Milan in 1902. His enthusiasm for Weber is reflected in all three overtures and their dramatic impact is in fact strengthened by his unerring ear for classical proportion.

Overture: Oberon

5 August 1952
all other details as above

A performance of great charm and delicacy, quite out-of-the-ordinary: excellent sound.

Overture: Der Freischütz

25 May 1945
NBC
Studio 8H
NCRA

3 January 1952
NBC
Carnegie Hall
Ger/It AT 116

One of the great works of German Romanticism given, on both occasions, performances which fully reveal the lyric and dramatic qualities of the music.

WOLF-FERRARI, Ermanno

Overture: Il Segreto di Susanna

10 March 1921
La Scala Orch.
Camden NJ
NCRA

The humour and vitality of the performance are evident in spite of the archaic sound. It is a pity that Toscanini did not re-record this delightful piece during his NBC days.

A GENERAL NOTE
on earlier editions released by
RCA, EMI and Decca

Many Toscanini records appear on dealers' second-hand lists and in shops specialising in deleted material.

Conditions will play a major part in the pricing of these discs, and having heard literally dozens, I can attest that remarkable results can be obtained if the correct cleaning agent, when needed, is used. The Zeepa Disk Masks has proved *very* successful in reducing surface noise and freshening the sound.

The following is a note on each of the companies' editions, which have appeared in the United Kingdom, with a mention of American LM editions etc.

RCA (RB's and VCM Boxes) Victor VIC & VICS	These are excellent, particularly the VCM Boxes and the VIC (not stereo simulated). The boxes are very consistent and contain at least one item that is unique: the 'Haffner' Symphony (November 4th 1946) is completely natural, rather dry, but not enhanced with echo that trails through endless empty halls! The stereo transfers were successful up to a point. The better the reproducing equipment the better the results obtained.
RCA/Camdens	All are long deleted, but are honest transfers of the original 78s.
RCA (American Victor LM's)	Many of these were sampled and proved very good indeed (prices vary from 3 or 4 dollars to 35 dollars for a rare item). I would suggest the reader try any he can obtain, but again carefully cleaning before playing will make all the difference.
Reader's Digest	Issued as a 10-record set, containing over 50 items. Stereo and mono editions were released. There is very little to choose between them, as both are in excellent sound. Well worth getting.
HMV (EMI Records)	On ALP, BLP and CSLP there appeared 110 items on 70 records: by any standards a real tribute to the artistry of Toscanini. Unfortunately they vary alarmingly: when good they are wonderful (Saint-Saëns 3rd Symphony), when poor they are fuzzy and confused (Pines and Fountains).

168

JAP 100	A complete edition of every RCA recording (even the elusive Brunswicks are included), and also items never put on to lp, such as Haydn Symphony 98, the 1941 Brahms 1st, the 1939 *Eroica* and Leonore nos 2 and 3 Overtures, Beethoven no. 8 etc. This is available direct from JVC (RCA Japan) but will at any time go out of print only to be released again, perhaps, a year later. This is the indispensable set for any serious Toscanini collector.
'Private' labels	Many Toscanini performances published under private labels are of considerable interest and value to dedicated collectors, but it is clearly not possible to comment on their quality as standards vary a great deal. However, a careful watch on the second-hand market can still yield rich dividends.

1982 Special RCA edition

At a reception given in Venice on 11 January 1982 attended by the President of the Italian Republic, RCA announced an important new series of re-issues of Toscanini's recordings to commemorate the 25th anniversary of his death. All the recordings have been completely re-mastered by E.Di Giuseppe and G.Di Toma under the supervision of Benito Vassura, Classical Director of RCA Italy.

As this book goes to press details of the first 20 releases have been made available: for further information please refer to the appropriate entries in the Selected Discography.

VL 4600	RESPIGHI	
	Fountains of Rome	(17 Dec 1951)
	Feste Romane	(12 Dec 1949)
	Pines of Rome	(17 Mar 1953)
VL 4601	BEETHOVEN	
	Symphony no 5	(22 Mar 1952)
	Symphony no 7	(9 Nov 1951)
VL 4602	BEETHOVEN	
	Symphony no 9 ('Choral')	(31 Mar/1 Apr 1952)
VL 4603	MOZART	
	Symphony no 40 in G minor	(12 Mar 1950)
	SCHUBERT	
	Symphony no 8 in B minor ('Unfinished')	(12 Mar 1950)
VL 4604	ROSSINI Overtures	
	Barber of Seville	(28 Jun 1945)
	La Cenerentola	(28 Jun 1945)
	Semiramide	(28 Sep 1951)
	William Tell	(19 Jan 1953)
	Il Signor Bruschino	(8 Jun 1945)
	La Gazza Ladra	(8 Jun 1945)
VL 4605	VERDI	
	Rigoletto, Act IV	(25 May 1944)
	Hymn of the Nations	(8 and 10 Dec 1943)
	Te Deum (from 'Four Sacred Pieces')	(14 Mar 1954)

VL 4606	VERDI Overtures	
	La Forza del Destino	(10 Nov 1952)
	Luisa Miller	(25 Jul 1943)
	I Vespri Siciliani	(24 Jan 1942)
	ROSSINI Overtures	
	L'Italiana in Algeri	(14 Apr 1950)
	L'Assiedo di Corinto	(14 Jun 1945)
VL 4607	SMETANA	
	Moldau (from 'Ma Vlast')	(19 Mar 1950)
	SIBELIUS	
	Finlandia	(5 Aug 1952)
	SUPPÉ	
	Overture: Poet and Peasant	(18 Jul 1943)
	SAINT-SAËNS	
	Danse Macabre	(1 Jun 1950)
VL 4608	WAGNER	
	Die Walküre: Act I, scene 3	(22 Feb 1941)
	Ride of the Valkyries	(3 Jan 1952)
	Forest Murmurs	(29 Oct 1951)
	Siegfried Idyll	(29 Jul 1952)
VL 4609	WAGNER	
	Tristan: Prelude and Liebestod	(7 Jan 1952)
	Parsifal: Prelude and Good Friday Spell	(22 Dec 1949)
VL 4610 (2)	VERDI	
	Requiem	(27 Jan 1951)
VL 4620 (7)	BEETHOVEN	
	Symphony no 1	(21 Dec 1951)
	Symphony no 2	(7 Nov 1949 / 5 Oct 1951)
	Symphony no 3 (Eroica)	(6 Dec 1953)
	Symphony no 4	(3 Feb 1951)
	Symphony no 5	(22 Mar 1952)
	Symphony no 6 (Pastoral)	(14 Jan 1952)
	Symphony no 7	(9 Nov 1951)
	Symphony no 8	(10 Nov 1952)
	Symphony no 9 ('Choral')	(31 Mar / 1 Apr 1952)
	Overtures:	
	Leonore no 3	(1 June 1945)
	Coriolan	(1 Jun 1945)
	Prometheus	(18 Dec 1944)
	Egmont	(19 Jan 1953)
	Fidelio	(10 Dec 1944)
	Consecration of the House	(16 Dec 1947)
VL 4624	LA SCALA	

VL 4624   LA SCALA
A collection of Toscanini's early acoustic recordings, details of which may be found in the Selected Discography under Beethoven, Berlioz, Bizet, Donizetti, Massenet, Mozart, Pizzetti, Respighi and Wolf-Ferrari.

INDEX

Illustrations indicated in bold type

Agate, James 107
Aldrich, Richard 27, 29, 32, 39, 40
Alexandria 63
Alfano, Franco 42
Antek, Samuel 79
Atterberg, Karl
 – Symphony no 6 114

Bach, Johann Sebastian 112, 128
 – B Minor Mass 62
 – St. Matthew Passion 62
Barber, Samuel 128
 – Adagio for Strings 82
Barbirolli, Sir John 10, 66, 77, 79
Barcelona 16, 34
Bartók, Bela 112
Bayreuth 20, 21, 29, 48-57, 60, 69, 105
BBC Choral Society 71
BBC Symphony Orchestra
 9, 10, 41, 54, 63, 66, 68, 71-4, 81, 85, 98,
 103, 105, 110, 118-9
Beecham, Sir Thomas 8, 66, 98, 108-10
Beethoven, Ludwig van
 8, 9, 17, 32, 41, 47, 65, 70, 71, 74, 85,
 100, 103, 107, 108, 116, 121, 128-35
 – Fidelio 14, 47, 57-9, 86, 117
 – Grosse Fuge 72
 – Missa Solemnis 62, 72-3, 90, 119, 122
 – Overture: Coriolan 103
 – Overture: Leonore no 2 94
 – Overture: Leonore no 3 59, 119
 – Overture: Zur Weihe des Hauses 100
 – Piano Concerto no 3 84
 – Piano Concerto no 5 ('Emperor') 84
 – Piano Sonata in B flat, op 106
  ('Hammerklavier') 72, 100
 – Septet 86
 – String Quartet in F, op 135 72
 – Symphony no 1 71, 94
 – Symphony no 2 72
 – Symphony no 3 (Eroica)
  38, 41, 54, 65-6, 70, 72, 81-2, 105, 112,
  119
 – Symphony no 4 72, 105
 – Symphony no 5 40, 86
 – Symphony no 6 (Pastoral) 63, 71, 100, 122
 – Symphony no 7
  56, 69, 70, 86, 90, 105, 107, 119

 – Symphony no 8 72, 121
 – Symphony no 9 ('Choral')
  32, 39, 40, 71, 72
 – Violin Concerto 82
Belasco, David 30, **34**
Bellini, Vincenzo
 – I Capuleti ed i Montecchi 34
 – Norma 20, 110, 114
Berg, Alban
 – Lulu 113
 – Wozzeck 113
Berlin 48, 50-2, 110
Berlin Philharmonic Orchestra 8, 66
Berliner Tagblatt 48
Berlioz, Hector 114, 136
 – Faust 62, 70
 – Romeo and Juliet 108
 – Symphonie Fantastique 114
Bizet, Georges 137
 – Carmen 24, 29, 35
Bliss, Sir Arthur 105
Bloch, Ernest 41, 107
Boccherini, Ridolfo
 – Minuet in A 86
Boito, Arrigo
 19, 20, 33, 38, 42-3, 62, 93, 95, 137
 – Mefistofele
  19, 26, 32, 38, 41, 43, 62, 93, 107
 – Nerone 33, 38, 42-3
Bologna 16-7, 23, 41, 50, 55, 93
Bolzoni, Giovanni 16
Bonavia, Ferruccio 52, 108
Boston 82
Boston Symphony Orchestra 50, 65, 66
Boult, Sir Adrian
 7, 9, 19, 64, 66, 68, 72, 96, 98, 103, 111, 120
Brahms, Johannes
 8, 12, 23, 65, 73, 76, 86, 101, 116, 138-141
 – Double Concerto 84
 – Piano Concerto no 2 82
 – Requiem 61, 71
 – 'St. Antoni' Variations 74, 76, 82
 – Symphony no 1 12, 63, 70, 74, 79, 105,
  119
 – Symphony no 2 65
 – Symphony no 3 76, 93
 – Symphony no 4 54, 66, 68, 76
 – Tragic Overture 19, 71, 74, 76, 88, 116

Brain, Dennis 76, 86
Brazil 101
ss *Bremen* 83
Briga 94
Budapest 60
Buenos Aires 21-5, 47, 55, 85
– Teatro Colón 32
Burghauser, Hugo 56
Busch, Adolf 73
Busch, Fritz 73, 77
Busoni, Ferruccio 12, 30, 103
– Rondo Arlecchinesco 70
Busseto 33, 101
Cairo 63
Camden, Archie 73
Camden, New Jersey 40
Cameron, Basil 55
Campanini, Cleofonte 23
Cantelli, Guido 101
Cardus, Neville 76, 107, 108
Carnegie Hall **81**, 89, 90, 120
Caruso, Enrico 25-7, 29, 33
Casa Verdi 101
Casale Monferrato 16
Casella, Alfredo 7
Castelbarco, Count 20
Castelbarco, Emanuela **75**
Catalani, Alfredo 16, 23, 141
– *Edmea* 16
– *Loreley* 16
– *La Wally* 16
Chaliapin, Feodor 26, 32
Charpentier, Gustave
– *Louise* 24
Cherubini, Luigi 70, 141
– Overture: Anacreon 68, 100
Chicago 82
Chicago Opera 43
Chotzinoff, Samuel 79, 110, 121
Cimarosa, Domenico 142
Cologne 41
Columbia 54
Cooley, Carlton 90, **120**
Copland, Aaron
– El Salón México 82
Corelli, Arcangelo 38
Coronaro, Gaetano 27
Corriere della sera 42
Covent Garden 64, 74
Cowan, Robert 126

The Daily Telegraph 108
Dallas **109**
Damrosch, Walter
– *Cyrano* 35
Davenport, Marcia 116-7
Debussy, Claude
8, 12, 26, 30, 38, 62, 107, 142
– L'Après-midi 23
– Iberia 38, 40, 70-1
– La Mer 30, 62, 69, 70, 82, 93, 113
– *Pelléas et Melisande* 24, 26, 47, 62, 114

Decca 168-9
Depanis, Giuseppe 17, 30
Destinn, Emmy 27
Didur, Adamo 32
Deppel, Andreas 27
Dixie 88
Dollfuss, Engelbert 57
Donizetti, Gaetano 142
– *Lucia di Lammermoor* 48
Dorfmann, Ania 84
Dresden 52
Dukas, Paul 143
– *Ariane et Barbe-bleue* 30, 113
Dvořák, Antonin 23, 143
Dyment, Christopher 126

Eames, Emma 29
Einaudi, Luigi 101
Elgar, Sir Edward 8, 30, 66, 69, 143
– Enigma Variations 23, 65, 69, 113
EMI 94, 168-9
Elmendorff, Karl 54
Esterházy 116
Excelsior 50

Farrar, Geraldine 20, 29, 35, 38
Fascists 39, 41, 43, 50, 55, 63, 77, 93
Ferrari, Pompeo 110
Feuermann, Emmanuel 72
Figner, Nicolai 16
Florence 95
Franchetti, Alberto
– *Cristoforo Colombo* 21
Franck, Cesar 144
– Les Eolides 100
Frankfurter Zeitung 48
Fremstad, Olive 29
Fürtwangler, Wilhelm
8, 47, **51**, 58, 62, 66, 71, 77, 103, 107, 122

Galeotti, Cesare
– *Anton* 21
Gallignani, Giuseppe 43
Gatti-Casazza 20, 26-7, 30, 34, **34**, 35
Gavazzeni, Gianandrea 43
Genoa 16, 21
Gershwin, George 82, 144
– An American in Paris 82
– Rhapsody in Blue 73
Gervais, T W 108, 120
Ghiringhelli, Antonio 99, 100
Gilman, Lawrence 111-2
Giovinezza 41-3, 50, 55, 65
Gingold, Joseph 79, 80
Giordano, Umberto 34
Giulini, Carlo Maria 30
Glinka, Mikhail 144
Gluck, Alma 116
Gluck, Christoph Willibald 144
– *Orfeo* 24, 29, 116
The 'Gluepot' 119
Glyndebourne 73

Goodman, Benny 73
Goossens, Eugene 65
- Sinfonietta 65
Gould, Glenn 115
Gounod, Charles
- *Faust* 84
Griswold, Putman 32
Grofé, Ferde 82, 145
- Grand Canyon Suite 82
Grove's Dictionary of Music and Musicians
 (5 ed) 108
Grubicy, Vittore 110
Gustavson, Eva 87

Haggin, B H 79, 85
Harris, Roy
- Symphony no 3 82, 114
Haydn, Joseph 8, 108, 116, 145-6
- Symphony no 88 in G 81
- Symphony no 92 in G ('Oxford') 63
- Symphony no 98 in B flat 86
- Symphony no 101 in D ('Clock') 9, 44,
 48-9

Heifetz, Jascha 82
Hempel, Freida 30, 32
Henderson, W J 29
Henschel, Sir George 65, 111
Henschel, Helen 65, 71, 111
Hérold, Louis 146
Hess, Dame Myra 84, 96, 98, 109, 117
Hindemith, Paul 112
Hitler, Adolf 9, 41, 55
Homer, Louise 30, 32
Honegger, Arthur
- Pacific 231 113
Horowitz, Sonia 11, **13**
Horowitz, Vladimir 66, 82
Horzowski, Mieczylaw 84
Howes, Frank 107
Huberman, Bronislaw 56, **62,** 63
Humperdinck, Englebert 146

Isola Madre 96
Isola San Giovanni 94-8

Jerusalem 63
Jörn, Carl 32

Kabalevsky, Dmitri 146
Kahn, Otto 34-5
Karajan, Herbert von 48, 58, 62, 74
Karlsruhe 50
Keeffe, Bernard 107
Keller, Hans 77
Kennedy, Lauri 85
Kipnis, Alexander 29, 51-2, 58, 60
Kleiber, Erich **51**
Klemperer, Otto
 7, 41, **51,** 56, 71, 103, 105, 122
Knappertsbusch, Hans 54
Kodály, Zoltan **45,** 60-1, 146

- *Psalmus Hungaricus* 61
- Symphony in C 61
Koussevitsky, Serge 66, 68, 105, 115
Krauss, Clemens 57
Kreisler, Fritz 40-1
Krips, Josef 104
Kullman, Charles 60

Lago Maggiore **95,** 96
Legge, Walter 74, 76, 94
Lehmann, Lotte 56, **56, 57,** 58, 60, 117, 119
Leinsdorf, Erich 58
Leipzig 18
Leoncavallo, Ruggiero
- *I Pagliacci* 17, 38
Liadov, Anatol 147
Lipatti, Dinu 94
Life magazine 11
The Listener 52
London
 12, 50, 53, 63-5, 73-4, 77, 79, 81, 84, 90,
 94, 98, 100, 103, 120
London Music Festival 66, 70, 72
London Philharmonic Orchestra 66
London Symphony Orchestra 64
Long, Marguerite 63
Lucerne 53, 62, 74, 77, 94, 114
ss Lusitania 35

Mace, Ralph 126
Madison Square Garden 86
Mahler, Alma 29
Mahler, Gustav 8, 23, 29
- Symphony no 5 23
Mann, Thomas **54**
Mapleson, Lionel 31
Marsh, Robert 40, 114-5
Martinelli, Giovanni 35
Martini, Carla de 20, 22
 (*see also Toscanini, Carla*)
Martucci, Giuseppe 16, 23, 38, 50, 55, 82
- Piano Concerto 84
Mascagni, Pietro
- *Iris* 35
Mascheroni, Edoardo 34
Mase, Georgina and Owen 103
Massenet, Jules 147
- *Manon* 30
McNaught, William 118
Meiningen Orchestra 116
Melchior, Lauritz **83**
Mendelssohn, Felix 18, 147-8
Mengelberg, Wilhelm 46, 103
Menuhin, Yehudi 82, **98,** 109
Merriman, Nan 86
The Met (*see under New York Metropolitan*
 Opera)
Miguez, Leopoldo 15
Milan
 16, 21, 23, 27, 34, 38-9, 42, 47-8, 79, 93,
 95, 99-101, 110
- Conservatory 38, 43

173

– Teatro Dal Verme 16, 38
– Via Durini 95
  (see also La Scala)
Milanov, Zinka 72-3, 86
Miller, Frank 90
Minetti, Enrico 93
Mitropoulos, Dmitri 93, 113
Moldovan, Nicolas **120**
Mont, Willem de 119
Montani, Paolina 11
Monto Santo 38
Monte, Toti dal 41
Monteux, Pierre 7, 41, 79
Montemezzi, Italo 30, 33
– L'Amore dei Tre Re 30, 33
Montevideo 23, 55, 85
Montreal 40
Moscona, Nicola 73, 86
Mossolov, Alexander
– Iron Foundry 114
Mozart, Leopold 148
Mozart, Wolfgang Amadeus
  8, 9, 17, 24, 47, 58, 60, 98, 103, 105, 112,
  149-50
– Bassoon Concerto in B flat, K191 84
– Don Giovanni 24, 47
– The Magic Flute 10, 14, 24, 47, 60, 72
– The Marriage of Figaro 24, 60
– Piano Concerto in B flat, K595 84
– Symphony no 35 in D ('Haffner') 48-9,
  103
– Symphony no 39 in E flat 112
– Symphony no 40 in G minor
  30, 66, 70, 79-81, 105
– Symphony no 41 in C ('Jupiter') 86
Muck, Karl 51-2
Mugnone, Leopoldo 23, 108
The Musical Times 108-9, 118
Mussolini, Benito
  9, 39, 41-2, 44, 49, 55, 57, 86, 93
Mussorgsky, Modest 150
– Boris Godunov 29, 32, 41, 113-4

Napoleon 41
Nash, Heddle 70
National Anthems 66, 74
National Gallery Concerts 84
NBC Symphony Orchestra
  10-11, 17, 27, 70, 73, 76-7, 79-82, 85-8,
  90-1, 94-5, 101, 104, 111, 113-4, 119-20
Nazis 23, 55, 57, 77
Nelli, Herva 87
Newman, Ernest 52, 54, 60, 69, 107
New York
  11-12, 27, 29-30, 32-3, 35, 39, 46, 50,
  55-6, 66, 77, 79, 87, 93, 95-6, 101, 117
New York Metropolitan Opera
  20, 25-7, 29-35, 38-9, 43, 47-8, 55, 86,
  111, 116
New York Philharmonic-Symphony
  Orchestra
  10, 27, 44, 47-9, **49,** 50, 55, 64-8, 77, 79,
  82, 85-6, 89, 98, 103, 109, 114
New York Herald Tribune 32
New York Times 27, 32, 90
Nissen, Hans Hermann 117

Ormandy, Eugene 85
Oxford 63

Paderewski, Ignacy 41
Padua 38
Paganini, Nicolo 151
O Pais 16
Palermo 17
Palestine 114
Palestine Symphony Orchestra **62,** 63, 77
Pallanza 96
Paris 50, 62-4, 74, 77, 79, 94, 114
Parma 11, 12, **14,** 21
– Conservatory 12, 14-5
– Teatro Regio 12, 14, 90
Parry, Sir Hubert 23
Pataky, von 73
Peerce, Jan 86-7
Pertile, Aureliano 41
Petri, Egon 104
Philadelphia 114
Philadelphia Orchestra 10, 50, 85
Philharmonia Orchestra 74, 76, 86, 94, 111
Pini-Corsi, Antonio 17
Pisa 17
Pittsburgh 82
Pizzetti, Ildebrando 151
– Débora e Jaèle 44
Polacco, Giorgio 34
Pomé, Alessandra 17
Ponchielli, Amilcare
– Dance of the Hours 86
Prague 60
Prokofiev, Sergei 151
Puccini, Giacomo
  8, 12, 19, 30, **31, 34,** 42, 44, 93, 110, 151
– La Bohème 18-9, 30, 42, 87
– La Fanciulla del West 31
– Gianni Schicchi (see also Trittico) 64
– Manon Lescaut 30, 42, 64, 93
– La Rondine 101
– Tosca 21, 30, 34
– Trittico operas 42, 64
– Turandot 42, 64, 114

Queen's Hall 8, 10, 64-6, 70-1, 73-4, 98, 119
Quisca **39**

Rachmaninoff, Sergei **61**
Radio City 10, 79
Radio Corporation of America (RCA)
  79, 168-9
The Radio Times 103
Raff, Joachim 86
Ravel, Maurice 50, 62, 152
– Bolero 50, 62
– Daphnis and Chloe Suite no 2 63

- Piano Concerto for the Left hand 63
The Record Guide 112
Recordings
  (*see Selected Discography pp 128 et seq*)
Red Cross 86
Rees, C B 103
Reining, Maria 94
Respighi, Ottorino 70, 112, 152
- The Fountains of Rome 40
- The Pines of Rome 44
Ricordi, Giulio 20-2, 34, 104-5
Rimington's Review 68
Rio de Janeiro 15-6, 20, 71, 85
Robinson, Edward 103
Rodzinski, Artur 77, 79
Rome 23
- Augusteum 38
Ronald, Sir Landon 69
Rosé, Arnold 58
Rosenfield, John 87
Rosi, Lelio 14, 16
Rossini, Gioacchino 8, 86, 93, 107, 152-4
- *La Gazza Ladra* 93
- *Mose* 93
Royal Albert Hall 64-5, 98
Royal Festival Hall 74-6, 90
Royal Opera House 66
Royal Philharmonic Orchestra 98
Royal Philharmonic Society 64, 66
Russia 74

Sabata, Victor de 120
Sacchi, Filippo 10, 12, 43
Sachs, Harvey 10, 19, 30, 35, 41, 43, 47, 90
Saint-Saëns, Camille 154
Salzburg
  10, 48-9, 54, 56-62, 77, 79, 94, 96, 114,
  117
San Francisco **113**
Sao Paulo 85
Sarnoff, David 79
La Scala
  11, 17-21, 23-27, 29, 32-3, 35, 39, 40-44,
  46, 48-50, 55, 57-8, 62, 64, 74, 79, 82,
  86-7, 93-5, 99, 101, 104, 110, 112, 114,
  115, 120
La Scala Orchestra
  41, 43, 50, 64, 74, 85, 95, 99, 101
Schnabel, Arthur 100
Schoenbach, Sol 85
Scholes, Percy 110
Schubert, Franz 155-6
- Symphony no 9 ('Great') 18-9, 105, 116
Schumann, Robert 94, 103
Schwarz, Rudolf 50
Scott, Norman 87
Serafin, Tullio 35
Shaw, Robert 107, 109
Shore, Bernard 69, 71-2, 85
Shostakovich, Dmitry 156
- Symphony no 1 70, 82
- Symphony no 7 ('Leningrad') 82

Sibelius, Jean 8, 114, 156-7
- En Saga 23, 72, 113-4
- Swan of Tuonela 44, 114
- Symphony no 2 72, 114, 119
- Symphony no 4 114
- Symphony no 5 114
- Symphony no 7 66, 114
Sibelius Society 66
Smart, Sir George 71
Smetana, Bedrich 157
- Vltava (Ma Vlast) 100
Smith, John Stafford 157
Smith, Max 111
Sousa, John Philip 157
- Stars and Stripes 86
Spetrino, Francesco 30
Stabile, Mariano 41, 58, 96
Stanford, Sir Charles Villiers 23
Steinbach, Fritz 116
Stockholm 63, 77
Stokowski, Leopold 82, 85
Storchio, Rosina 20, 38
Strauss, Johann 157-8
Strauss, Richard 8, 23-4, 32, 56, 158-9
- *Arabella* 56
- Domestic Symphony 23
- Don Juan 23, 100
- Don Quixote 72, 90
- *Salome* 23
- Till Eulenspiegel 22, 32, 113, 116
Stravinsky, Igor 113
Stresa 96
Studio 8-H 10, 81
Sullivan, Sir Arthur 23
The Sun 29
Suppé, Franz von 159
'Symphony of the Air' 91
Szell, George 8

Tamagno, Francesco 21
Taubman, Howard 10, 27, 62, 86, 110, 112
Tchaikowsky, Peter Ilych 23, 159
- *Eugene Onegin* 21, 113
- Piano Concerto no 1 66, 82
Tel-Aviv 63
Tenda 94
The Hague 63, 77
The Times 60, 68-9, 90, 107
Thode, Madame **57**
Thomas, Ambroise 160
Thorborg, Kerstin 73
Thurston, Frederick 74
Tintner, Georg 59
Tommasini, Vincenzo 38, 43, 82
- Carnival of Venice 70
Toscanini
- Carla **35, 44, 67, 84,** 96-7
- Claudio 11-2
- Paolina 11
- Walfredo **88, 99**
- Wally 20, **35, 44,** 74, 99, 100
- Walter **22, 88,** 101

175

– Wanda **28**
Tovey, Sir Donald 103, 105
Treviso 17
Troubetskoy **89**
Tucker, Richard 87
Turin 16-20, 23, 30, 39, 42, 47, 50, 116
– Teatro Regio 16-7
Turner, W J 65

US Office of War Information 86

Valdengo, Giuseppe 87
Vaughan Williams, Ralph
– Tallis Fantasia 72
– Symphony no 6 74
Venice
– Teatro la Fenice 94, 99, 100
Verdi, Giuseppe
8, 9, 11-2, 14, 16-7, 19-24, 29, 32-3, 41,
86, 88, 90, 93, 95, 103-05, 112, 116, 120,
160-3
– *Aida*
12, 15-6, 20, 27, 29, 34, 48, 71, **87**, 87, 91,
117
– *Un Ballo in Maschera*
11, 17, 23, 33, 87, 90, 91, 117
– *Don Carlos* 12
– *Falstaff*
10, 17, 19, 20, 33, 38, 40-1, 48, 57-8, 60,
73-4, 87, 96, 101, 108, 117
– *La Forza del Destino* 17, 74
– Hymn of the Nations 74, 86
– *Macbeth* 73
– *Nabucco* 93, 101
– *Otello* 17, 19, 21, 87, 108, 112, 120, 125
– *Requiem*
8, 21, 30, 32-3, 57, 61, 72, 82, 98, 101,
105-6, 108, 112
– *Rigoletto* 30, 41, 48, 86, 95
– Te Deum (from 'Four Sacred Pieces')
21, 72, 91, 93
– *La Traviata*
21, 33, 38, 87-8, 101, 112, 117
– *Il Trovatore* 21, 34, 48, 104
Verona 16
Victor 54
Vienna 48, 50, 56-8, 60, 62, 114
Vienna Philharmonic Orchestra
56, 58, 59, 60, 62-3
Vienna State Opera 57
Vivaldi, Antonio 107

Votto, Antonino 44, 93

Wagner, Cosima 21, 57
Wagner, Friedelind 110
Wagner, Richard
8, 12, 14, 16-7, 19-24, 29, 32, 38, 41, 51-2,
54, 58, 60, 69, 70, 74, 77, 86, 91, 101,
103, 111, 115-7, 163-66
– A Faust Overture 32, 69
– *The Flying Dutchman* 17
– 'Forest Murmurs' 82
– *Die Götterdämmerung*
17, 20, 29, 32, 38, 44, 52, 69, 116
– *Lohengrin* 14, 21, 63, 104
– *Die Meistersinger*
9, 10, 12, 20, 41, 44, 47, 52, 55, 58-9, 77,
91, 94, 107, 117
– *Parsifal* 47, 51, 54-5, 69, 105
– 'The Ride of the Valkyries' 82
– The *Ring* cycle 53
– *Siegfried* 21
– Siegfried Idyll 51-2
– *Tannhäuser* 49-52, 54, 62, 91
– *Tristan*
16, 19, 21, 23, 29, 32, 43, 47, 49-54, 107
– *Die Walküre* 21
Wagner, Siegfried
21, 29, 43, 48, 51-2, 55, 110
Wagner, Winifred 55
Wallenstein, Alfred 89
Walther Straram Orchestra 62
Walter, Bruno
7, 29, **51, 54**, 56, 58, **59**, 60, 66, 68, 80,
109, 122
Waldteufel, Emile 167
– The Skaters Waltz 86
Weber, Carl Maria von 167
– *Euryanthe* 23, 34, 44
– *Der Freischütz* 14
– Invitation to the Dance 72
Weingartner, Felix 7, 56, 58, 70, 72, 108
Westrup, J A 69
Wild, Earl 73
Wittgenstein, Paul 63
Wolf-Ferrari, Ermanno 30, 167
– *La Donne Curiose* 30
Wood, Sir Henry 54, 66
Woodgate, Leslie 71, 98

Zürich 94
Zweig, Stefan **59**